Law and the Economy

ROGER BOWLES

Martin Robertson · Oxford

First published in 1982
by Martin Robertson & Company Ltd.,
108 Cowley Road, Oxford OX4 1JF.

British Library Cataloguing in Publication Data

Bowles, Roger A.
   Law and the economy.
   1. Great Britain—Economic policy—1945-
   I. Title
   344.103'7   KD5295

ISBN 0-85520-465-6
ISBN 0-85520-474-5   Pbk

Phototypeset in 11 on 12pt English Times by
Getset (BTS) Ltd, Eynsham, Oxford
Printed and bound in Great Britain by
Billings, Worcester

To Sue

Contents

Tables and Figures

Preface

A book about Law and the Economy can be written in various ways and aimed at various audiences. My aim here has been primarily to show how modern economics can be fairly straightforwardly used to illuminate a number of legal problems. I have assumed that the reader knows very little about either economics or law, although I hope that there will be something here to interest those with some expertise in either, or even both, fields.

The first three chapters outline most of the economic theory that is needed to understand the remainder of the work. Those familiar with economics may fairly confidently skip these chapters, but those unfamiliar with it may find later sections a bit difficult in parts if they omit them.

As far as chapters 4 – 12 are concerned, it is perhaps well to emphasise that they are written from an economic standpoint. This has the consequence that the treatment is quite different from the one offered in most legal texts. My object is not to work systematically through a variety of doctrines or a series of cases and to build up a rationale as I go. Rather, my aim is to try and identify the major issues in an area and to discuss the law 'from a distance' as being just one institutional form that can be used to tackle problems. Although the result may appear to be rather discursive and eclectic in parts, not to say presumptuous, I have at least tried to follow a consistent path through the different areas.

I have tried throughout to avoid some of the deeper controversies surrounding the economic analysis of law.

There are major differences between groups of scholars over matters like the way in which law is to be interpreted. Some see it as the product of a ruling class anxious to protect their own interests whilst others see it as a response to pressures for the law to be economically efficient. Yet others, perhaps more conventionally, regard the development of law as reflecting a whole range of economic, social and political factors. Such disagreements are important to the extent that they provide competing perspectives from which law is to be viewed. Nevertheless, it is possible to apply economics to the law without being firmly committed to one or other view. It is clear that economic forces *are* relevant in shaping the law: whether they are, or should be, regarded as the primary or even the sole force is another matter. Our object here is simply to show that if economic arguments are to be taken seriously, there are significant implications for law and legal institutions.

One of the great obstacles to the absorption of economic thinking into the teaching of law, at least in England, seems to be that law courses are for the most part taught in a very 'technical' way. In order to penetrate such courses it will probably eventually be necessary for economists to arm themselves with a high degree of legal expertise and to write in a way that is directly geared to the demands of a specialist legal audience. At present it is probably fair to say that most lawyers find it difficult to see quite how they can make use of, or even sense of, much of the work done by economists on law. There are of course lawyers who are sympathetic to the contribution that economics and economists can make, and there are increasing signs of legal writers taking explicit account of economic arguments. There remains however considerable scope for further work on bridging the gaps between the disciplines.

As far as incorporating legal considerations into economics is concerned, the process seems to be well under way. The main difficulty as far as teaching goes is that much of the work that has been done is rather scattered, so that although much of this book is written in a way that will seem descriptive and low-brow to many economists, I hope that this work may be of some value to students of economics.

For economists and lawyers alike there can be little doubt that a deeper understanding of the way in which law affects and is affected by the economic environment will be of value all round. This book at least is based upon such a presumption although it represents very much a first step and is designed to stimulate the reader's appetite rather than to provide a definitive treatment of any or all of the issues upon which it touches. The guide to further reading at the end of each chapter should give the reader some idea about where to go next. Bon voyage.

Roger A. Bowles   Bath, April 1982

Acknowledgements

I must admit at once that I am not trained as a lawyer. Despite this handicap, I have for the past seven or so years been working on various legal problems and trying to bring economics to bear upon them. This work has been facilitated primarily by my links with the Social Science Research Council's Centre for Socio-Legal Studies in Oxford, and I owe a great debt to many of the staff and others associated with the Centre. In particular I would like to take this opportunity to thank Jenny Phillips and Chris Whelan with whom I have collaborated on various pieces of research. This collaboration has been most enjoyable.

I am indebted to the Universities of Nottingham and Bath for providing encouragement in the pursuit of what must seem a sometimes esoteric area of research. My thanks are due to undergraduates at Nottingham who in 1978/79 took a course on the Economics of Legal Policy as part of an option and to participants in the Summer School for lawyers wishing to learn economics organised by the SSRC at the University of York in the summer of 1978. I learned a great deal from teaching law and economics, and I would like to thank those involved for their patience and good humour.

Finally, I would like to thank those who have been directly concerned with the writing of this book. Michael Hay of Martin Robertson has been a considerable encouragement throughout; various anonymous referees have made most helpful comments and various of the staff in the Office of the School of Humanities and Social Sciences at the University of

Bath have at different times cheerfully and efficiently turned my 'spider writing' into typed form. Last, but by no means least, my wife Sue has put up very nicely with someone who was at times more busy and preoccupied than they might otherwise have been.

Table of Cases

1

An Introduction to
Economic Analysis

The pair of assertions upon which this book rests are firstly
that an understanding of law is furthered by an awareness of
the economic background against which it operates and
secondly that the discipline of economics is a useful guide to
how economies and their individual inhabitants work.
Neither assertion is without its critics, but rather than go to
great lengths to support these claims we will simply take them
as given and rely upon an evaluation of the quality and
empirical reliability of the conclusions thus derived as the
best test of whether or not the endeavour is a useful one. Our
approach is not, of course, the only way of investigating the
economic context of law or the effects that law has on the
economic environment. It would be perfectly possible to
avoid using contemporary economic theory altogether and to
rely upon intuition or commonsense alone, or to derive one's
thoughts about law from an ideological starting position that
differs from the essentially libertarian and capitalist
perspective of modern economics. Such approaches, with
their implied and sometimes overt rejection of the value of
market-based economics, have their adherents but also have
drawbacks.

The object of this first chapter is to explore in rather
general terms the ways in which economists have come to find
it expedient to characterise economic behaviour. Subsequent
chapters in the first part of the book take a more detailed
look at some of the elements of economics that are of
particular relevance whilst later parts are more concerned

with applications of economic thinking to a variety of what might loosely be termed 'legal issues'.

THE DEVELOPMENT OF ECONOMICS

Economics as a distinctive discipline has been in existence for some two centuries. The founding work is generally regarded as Adam Smith's *An Inquiry into the Causes of the Wealth of Nations*, which was first published in 1776. Following this lead developed a tradition of 'Political Economy' with writers such as David Ricardo and John Stuart Mill taking up the search for the principles underlying economic behaviour. Their search was broadly-based: they did not shy away from enquiring into the activities of government or into the sorts of criteria that might or even ought to be applied when deciding upon the rightness of different actions. The theories developed by some of these early political economists were of substantial intellectual and political importance, laissez-faire doctrines and the philosophical theory of Utilitarianism occupying a central place in the tradition.

Contemporary economists seem by contrast to be rather timid creatures for the most part. The merest hint of a 'value judgment' is often enough to attract professional criticism, austerity of method is something to be applauded and in many areas of economics technical wizardry is *de rigueur*. Cheap gibes apart, there is an explanation for the major transformation that has occurred in the mode of economic analysis. The philosophical theory of logical positivism developed by Popper and others in the earlier part of the twentieth century had a profound and lasting effect on economics. The subject became a scientific discipline in which the procedures followed by natural scientists came to be regarded as the model. Emphasis came to be put on the formulation and testing of refutable hypotheses, despite the obvious limitations on the capacity for running experiments on live economies. Whilst such developments did have the beneficial effect of making economists think more carefully and objectively, they also had some less attractive consequences.

The theory of Utilitarianism had come to play a quite significant role in economics, but it became clear that the notion of utility failed in some respects to match up to the demand for objectivity. It was realised that the utility levels enjoyed by different individuals could not be simply compared, and this discovery dealt a severe blow to the ability of economists to make anything more than very conservative observations about the consequences of implementing different sorts of policies. No longer could it be boldly asserted that the gains enjoyed by the beneficiaries of a policy change would be greater than the losses sustained by those adversely affected or vice versa. Economists, if you like, became agnostics. It is probably not surprising that the abandonment of cardinal utilitarianism following the logical positivist attack was accompanied by a major shift away from the analysis of government policy and legislation.

The reorientation of interests threw up two major concerns. *Macroeconomics*, the study of economic aggregates such as the level of unemployment and the rate of inflation, is concerned primarily with developing theories that lay a base for predicting the effects of, but not necessarily advocacy of, different macroeconomic policies. The emergence of macroeconomics as a distinctive part of economic theory owed much to the work of John Maynard Keynes who in his *General Theory of Employment, Interest and Money* published in 1936 argued that a system of markets might have poorer self-stabilising properties than had been traditionally supposed. At the other end of the spectrum *microeconomics* set out to put the analysis of the behaviour of individual consumers and firms onto a substantial foundation. This also has become an increasingly formalised affair as successive efforts have attempted to expunge the analysis of unscientific elements like cardinal utility.

In the rigorous intellectual climate of such developments, interest rather flagged in the analysis of government decision-making and related areas, whilst much energy was devoted to abstract, sometimes esoteric, concerns. More recently however the institutional background against which economic behaviour takes place has come to be taken increasingly seriously. The resurgence of interest in the legal background of economics is but one aspect of the reawakening of interest in institutions. Economic theories of voting behaviour and politics (some of which are reviewed by Whynes and Bowles, 1981) have been developed in recent years and comprise further evidence of the interest in the institutional framework.

It is probably fair to remark however that many academic lawyers, and *a fortiori* many practising lawyers, find much of the economic analysis of law puzzling, inaccessible and misinformed. Most economists working in the area may be tempted in unguarded moments to remark that lawyers are preoccupied with matters of detail and that they lack a thorough grasp of the sorts of problems with which law is designed to deal. These antagonisms can be attributed in part to differences in the subject matter of the disciplines of economics and law and in part to different methodologies, but they are probably not readily resoluble. With this in mind, a 'willing suspension of disbelief' on the part of legal readers is needed, particularly during the following sections which outline some of the main components of modern economic theory. As hinted earlier, it is only once the reader has some grasp of economics and has seen how it may illuminate familiar problems that he will be in a position to form a view about whether his preconceptions of the usefulness of economics were well-founded.

ECONOMIC ANALYSIS AND ECONOMIC MAN

The cornerstone of economic analysis is the behaviour of the individual. The actions of firms or governments for example can be traced back to the actions of consumers, of shareholders or of voters. It is the individual assuming these various guises who thus rather naturally represents the initial, and dominant, focus of economic theory. Without a reasonable account of how individuals respond to constraints and opportunities of different kinds there is little hope of being able to understand or predict the behaviour of any part of an economy. One of the major tasks of economics has therefore been the search for satisfactory ways of modelling individual behaviour. The outcome has been the creation of 'homo economicus', a man who acts in ways that have a degree of mutual consistency. It is of course rather easy to find people who object that it is folly to characterise human beings as perfectly rational, selfish creatures who cynically manipulate their environment in such ways as to maximise the personal gains that they derive from it. It is less easy to find people prepared to propose coherent alternatives. The object of these opening sections is to give some idea of the ways in which economists have come to find it useful to think about individual behaviour. Having assembled a sketch of the individual, it is possible to proceed to filling in some of the detail of the great variety of institutional structures confronting him. The individual is being constructed in an institutional vacuum and then being dropped into a world that contains goods and services, other individuals, private and public agencies, and inter alia (and most importantly for present purposes) a legal system.

The Individual as Consumer

At the heart of the economic model of behaviour lies the assumption that individuals, fully-informed of all the consequences of different actions open to them, can reach a decision about what to do. The individual is thus taken to be able to pose to himself questions of the kind: shall I spend my last 50 pence on a loaf of bread or a pint of beer? Shall I work hard tomorrow or not? Shall I drive home particularly carefully this evening? and in addition to be able to decide upon the answers. This process of introspection may take little or no conscious effort although obviously one might expect people to take more care over 'big' decisions than over trivial ones. The individual is taken to be making choices by reference to their consequences and his own view of the relative attractiveness of different sets of consequences. It is of central importance to note that it is the individual's own view of relative attractiveness that is taken to be the appropriate criterion for action. In this individualistic model, the assumption of 'rationality' has as a main requirement that the individual acts 'consistently' and will choose the same action repeatedly when confronted on different occasions by the same set of choices.

Expressed more technically the individual's tastes and preferences are taken to remain *constant* at least over the period to which the analysis is intended to apply. This is not to imply that consumers never alter their views, but rather that adjustments take place over the longer term. Thus if I buy beer rather than bread this evening then faced with a similar choice tomorrow evening I can be expected to choose the same option even though in ten years time I may opt for bread. In addition to tastes remaining constant there are a few other restrictions that are imposed.

First, individuals are generally assumed to *prefer more to less*: offered two loaves of bread or one the individual may be expected to opt for two provided that this has no effect on the other opportunities the consumer has. In a slightly more complex case, given a choice between two bundles of goods A and B, where A comprises 2 apples and 2 oranges and B comprises 3 apples and 2 oranges the individual may be expected to choose B.

Secondly, individuals' choices are assumed to exhibit *transitivity*. That is to say that if we consider three bundles of goods, A, B and C, offered to consumers at the same price, then if the individual claims to prefer A to B in a pairwise comparison and B to C similarly, then faced with a choice between A and C, he is assumed to opt for A. Associated with this restriction on the characteristics that we impose upon the structure of preferences is an assumption of *completeness*, namely that the individual confronted by any conceivable pair of alternatives A and B will always be able to make one or other of the following assertions: (i) I prefer A to B, (ii) I prefer B to A or (iii) I am indifferent between A and B.

This series of axioms lies at the base of the great bulk of economic theorising: from these apparently mild assumptions can be deduced a bewildering variety of conclusions. Perhaps it should be pointed out that the 'bundles of goods' referred to in the axioms can take the form of alternative courses of action, and that nothing is being said about why the individual prefers X to Y (or whatever) or about which are the characteristics of a good or the consequences of a course of action that the individual finds particularly attractive.

Knowing how the individual responds to hypothetical questions about whether he prefers X to Y is not quite the whole story. If we are to predict how the individual will actually behave, it is necessary to say something about what determines the range of options from amongst which he is choosing. That is to say that we have to specify the *constraints* under which the individual is working before it is possible to draw any firm conclusions. This is normally done by observing the budget that the consumer has and taking account of the possible combinations of purchases consistent with not exceeding this budget. To give an idea of the position, let us suppose that apples cost 5 pence per pound, and oranges cost 10 pence per pound and that fruit can if required be traded in fractions of a unit. If the individual has a budget of 20 pence to spend, all the possible combinations of apples and oranges he can buy are contained in the shaded triangle in figure 1.1. He may buy two pounds of oranges and no apples, or four pounds of apples and no oranges, or give the money away and consume nothing, to take but three extreme cases. Normally he will buy a mixture of the two goods.

Given the axioms set out earlier, it can be shown that there will generally be a single point, that lies on what in the diagram is referred to as the 'budget line', that the consumer prefers over all others available to him with a budget constraint of 20 pence. Once this point has been identified the problem is solved, for we have deduced the combination of goods that we may expect the consumer to choose.

In many instances, our interest may extend beyond simply identifying the decisions that the consumer will take in a purely static world: it is most likely that the absolute and/or relative prices of the two goods will change at some stage and that the consumer's budget will expand or contract for whatever reason. How will the consumer's behaviour respond to such changes? A change in either the size of the budget or in any of the prices will alter the location of the budget line, and thus alter the set of combinations of goods available to the consumer. If the price of apples in our example should

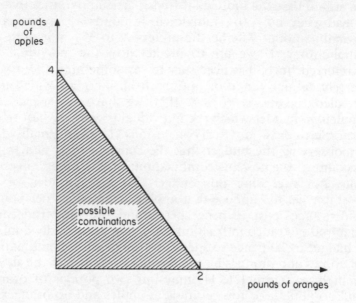

Figure 1.1 The Consumer's Choice Problem

double, then the budget line has to be redrawn in the way indicated in figure 1.2, and the combination of goods previously bought is no longer available. The consumer in such circumstances will switch to some new combination as indicated in the diagram.

It is well at this stage to say something about the notion of utility. In traditional economic theory, utility was used as a measure of the degree of well-being or satisfaction or welfare being derived by an individual consumer. Two different combinations of goods could be directly compared by a consumer who could at least in principle, assign a score of so many utils to each combination. This was useful because it enabled the economist to make assertions about whether projected changes altering the terms upon which goods were traded would leave the consumer better off or worse off and by how much. It has become clear however that the only legitimate things that may be said about consumers are of the kind: the consumer is better off as a result of a change if he can still achieve the position that he originally occupied but instead chooses to occupy a new position that was not originally available to him. This is a weak but exact definition of the circumstances under which a consumer may claim, or be inferred, to be better off, and it is a definition that does not rely in any way upon the notion of utility. Under this 'revealed preference' approach originally advanced by Samuelson it is possible to eliminate completely utility from economics. It is nevertheless very convenient for many purposes to retain the concept of utility, as we will now show.

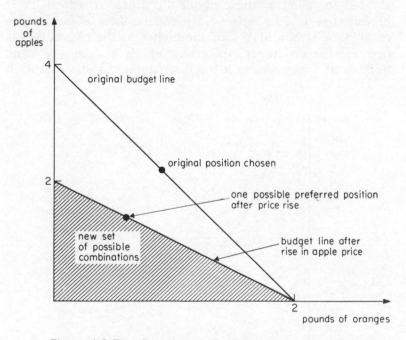

Figure 1.2 The Consumer's Response to a Price Rise

The fact that we require consumers to be able to impose a (well-behaved) binary ordering upon all combinations of goods (that is, that they can always say that they prefer A to B,

B to A, or are indifferent) allows us to define a particular level of utility as representing all combinations of goods between which the individual is indifferent. Thus a utility level, that we may label U_0, can be assigned to several combinations of apples and oranges. A level of utility, say U_1, can be assigned to those combinations generating a level of utility that is somewhat higher than U_0. Successive levels of well-being or utility can be depicted by the use of indifference curves: each indifference curve joins up all combinations of the two goods that yield a particular level of utility. The scale upon which utility is measured has no objective content, and thus we restrict ourselves to saying that a position on curve U_1 is preferred to a position on curve U_0 and to saying nothing about the degree to which U_1 is preferred to U_0. In figure 1.3 it can be seen by comparing combinations X and Y that the higher of the two curves is best for the consumer, since at point Y he gets the same number of oranges as at X but more apples. The assumption

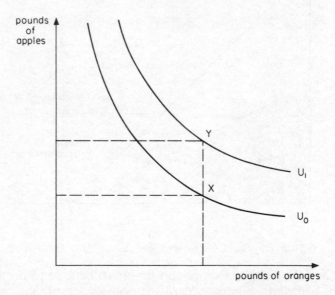

Figure 1.3 Utility Levels and Indifference Curves

that he prefers more to less is sufficient to infer that well-being along U_1 exceeds well-being along U_0.

It is but a short step from having derived indifference curves to show that a utility-maximising consumer's optimal position may be deduced by combining information about budgets and about preferences as encapsulated by indifference curves. Our analysis makes the conventional assumption that there is a bowing of the indifference curves towards the origin, or the zero, in the diagrams. This reflects the assumption of diminishing marginal utility which implies that as an individual is offered more of a commodity he has to be offered successively higher amounts of it to compensate for his loss of the other good or goods.

In figure 1.4 it is shown that a consumer who has a budget B is best advised to select combination of goods Z, for this is the combination within the limits of the budget that puts the consumer on the highest possible indifference curve or utility level. That is to say that there is no combination of apples

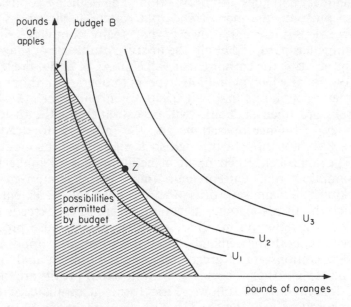

Figure 1.4 The Consumer's Point of Optimality

and oranges that will offer this consumer more satisfaction than the combination that he buys at Z unless his budget is increased. It is left to the reader to show that a change in the price of one or other of the goods will change both the level of well-being and the amounts of both goods that the consumer will buy.

Producers

We move now to the related question of the behaviour of sellers of products. Consumption activities cannot be maintained unless the goods and services are being both produced and sold. The same institutions or set of institutions will normally engage in both production and selling activities and, although many such institutions will be a specialist in one activity or the other, it is convenient here to consider both together. In the conventional story of the firm, an eagle-eyed entrepreneur spots a potentially profitable niche in the market, signs on workers, buys capital plant and machinery and goes into production. The resulting goods are then put onto the market and sold for the highest possible price. This picture is however not really complete, since nothing has been said about the mixture of the various inputs to production the entrepreneur will choose, or about the level of output at which he initially expects to operate or about the demand conditions that he expects to encounter. Until such details are filled in, banks will be extremely loathe to lend money to finance operations and the prospects for traders who have not thought through such matters will be modest.

The approach relied upon in economics is to make the assumption that entrepreneurs may be characterised as seeking to maximise profits. Profits represent the extent to which the firm's income, its revenue from sales, exceeds the costs of production incurred. In order to maximise profits therefore, both the demand conditions expected to apply and cost conditions are of great importance. From an analytical point of view, the procedure to be followed if profits are to be maximised runs as follows. First form an estimate of the number of units of the good that the firm might expect to sell at different price levels. Then estimate the lowest possible cost levels at which the firm can expect to achieve particular levels of production. It should now be possible to determine the level of output (which will generally have to be equal to the level of sales) at which profits are expected to be greatest. This level of output will have the property that it entails marginal revenue being equal to marginal cost. Marginal revenue refers to the additional revenue raised by expanding output by one unit whilst marginal cost refers to the increase in costs associated with the expansion of output by the same unit. At output below the profit-maximising level, marginal revenue will generally be greater than marginal cost whilst the reverse applies at output above the profit-maximising level.

The behaviour of marginal revenue at different output levels depends upon conditions in the product market in which the firm is operating whilst the structure of marginal cost will depend upon the technology used by the firm and by conditions prevailing in the markets upon which the firm buys its factors of production be they land, labour or capital. Without going into an elaborate taxonomy, it is useful to distinguish between monopoly and competition in product markets. In conditions of perfect competition the firm is characterised as being able to sell as much as it likes at the prevailing market price, say $\bar{p}$. The consequence is that marginal revenue will be constant at all levels of output, and equal to price $\bar{p}$. This is simply because if the firm produces an additional unit it will be able to sell this unit for a price $\bar{p}$. The reason for the market price being completely independent of the firm's output is that the latter is assumed to be very small in relation to the total supply of the good coming onto the market.

In conditions of monopoly on the other hand the firm is by assumption the only firm supplying the market. This has the effect of making market price depend upon the price charged by the firm: at high prices little will be demanded whilst at low prices more will be demanded by consumers. The firm this time has discretion over the price it charges: the firm is a 'price maker' by contrast with the firm in a competitive market which is a 'price taker'. When the monopolist is contemplating changing his output level he has to take account of the effect of the change in the price level at which he will now be selling all his units of production. If for example he knows that the market will absorb 100 units at £5 but only 99 units if the price rises to £5.10, he will calculate that the extra revenue associated with the hundredth unit of output is actually negative, since proceeds from selling 100 units are £500 whilst revenue from selling 99 units is £504.90. As will be shown in the discussion of the regulation of monopoly in chapter 11, the behaviour of a monopoly firm will be quite different from that of a competitive firm, even if both are operating under otherwise similar conditions.

Irrespective of market conditions however the profit-maximising rules remain the same: it is only the shape of the revenue schedules that differs. In either event the firm sets marginal revenue equal to marginal cost in order to determine the level of output: the competitive firm then offers the product for sale at the price determined by market forces whilst the monopolist sets a price which will enable him to sell just the amount he has produced. In both cases therefore the firm has now settled upon a complete, optimal, blue-print for its activities.

This idealised view of how firms behave has to be treated with some care. In particular, it has been implicitly assumed in our discussion of the competitive model that firms will be constrained by market forces to adopt a strategy of profit maximisation or otherwise fail to survive. In the longer term, any firms in a competitive market who produce at a level of cost that exceeds the lowest possible level will find themselves making a loss and will accordingly be forced out of business. It may also be observed that if, in the short run, some firms in the industry are managing to make a rate of return that is higher than the returns available elsewhere in the economy, new firms will be attracted into the industry. Equally if some firms are making losses then firms will start to leave the industry. In either case the number of firms will continue to vary until there are the right number of firms to ensure that the rate of return is brought into line with the one prevailing elsewhere.

There may be some occasions upon which firms have some

degree of protection from competitive forces. A firm may hold patents or franchises which make it difficult for new firms to enter a market. It is often argued that such barriers to entry into an industry will weaken the pressures on firms to follow the profit-maximising objective. Particularly if we replace the eagle-eyed entrepreneur by a large number of small shareholders in a company, it may be felt that the management, who are hired to represent the shareholders' interests, will be able to 'cheat'. A divorce between the ownership of a large firm and the controllers of its day-to-day activities may well give management and workers opportunities to pursue their own private interests at the expense of the firm's owners. Should the outcome of this however be that the firm becomes seriously inefficient, shareholders will sell their shares in the company, and the resulting fall in the share price will make the future acquisition of finance more difficult and thus impede expansion or it may encourage take-over by a more efficient firm which will introduce more profit-oriented management who will make more effective use of the firm's resources and assets.

It is possible to conclude that whilst profit maximisation is not necessarily an objective that firms pursue literally on all occasions, there will almost invariably be pressure on firms not to deviate too far from it. If this view is accepted, the most fruitful way of analysing particular firms or supply conditions generally in an industry is to assume simply that firms to set out to maximise profit. If profit maximisation were to be rejected as a plausible objective function, then something would have to be found to replace it. Despite the intuitive appeal of notions such as 'satisficing', an approach suggested by Simon (1959) under which firms are depicted as being concerned simply to ensure that they meet a succession of constraints or requirements imposed upon them rather than actively pursuing an open-ended goal of any kind, and of using objective functions containing variables other than profit, no convincing alternative that is generally applicable has as yet emerged.

Consumers, Producers and Market Price

The activities of buyers and sellers are mediated, at least in capitalist economies, by markets. The price that rules on the market acts as a signal to consumers and producers about the relative costs and rewards associated with buying and selling different commodities.

If the price of a good rises, it is to be expected that this will dampen consumer enthusiasm for it, but make it a more attractive thing to produce. Similarly a fall in price will deter producers but attract consumers. Price changes are not however an autonomous matter or an 'Act of God': they are directly precipitated by the actions of buyers and sellers. If sellers find it difficult to attract customers they will probably reduce prices to clear existing stocks and subsequently reduce their level of output. Consumers will respond to this price reduction by buying more of the good. The net result is that the downward drift of price will be halted as lower prices bring demand and supply into a closer match with one another.

Conversely, if sellers find that they are selling goods more rapidly than they anticipated, and consumers find it increasingly difficult to find traders who have sufficient stocks to meet their demands, then price will start to rise. The increase will continue up to the point at which demand has been choked off and extra production induced to an extent that is sufficient to once more match supply and demand.

Figure 1.5 illustrates the essence of the process. Price is initially 'too low' at p_1, but the excess demand at this price encourages sellers to continue raising price until an equilibrium is reached at p^*, where demand and supply are equal. Similarly, had price started 'too high' at p_2, competition to attract buyers would have forced price down to the so-called market-clearing level of p^*. The demand and supply curves from which these inferences about price adjustments are drawn can be thought of as representing the plans that consumers and producers have. Underlying the demand curve are calculations by consumers about how many apples or whatever they wish to buy at different apple prices. The relation between price and the quantity demanded is derived from the analysis of consumer behaviour outlined earlier and epitomised in figure 1.2. Holding the price of oranges constant and allowing apple prices to change it is possible to trace out how the consumer adjusts his demand for apples and oranges. By adding up the demands by individual consumers for apples at different apple prices it is possible to derive a downward sloping demand curve for apples of the kind illustrated in figure 1.5.

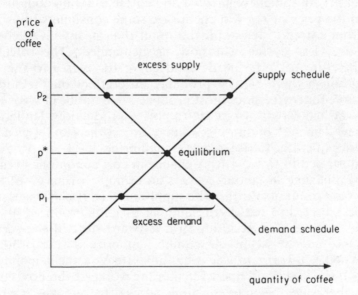

Figure 1.5 The Determination of Market Price

As far as producers are concerned, the supply curve represents the response that they will make when they discover what price the market sets, or is expected to set, for the product they sell. At different prices they will decide upon which is the profit-maximising level of production, a decision that will itself embody calculations about the volume of labour, materials and other inputs required.

Provided that demand and supply curves do not slope 'perversely' then there will exist a stable equilibrium price that markets may be expected to reach spontaneously. The curves are however drawn on the assumption of other things remaining equal (the so-called *ceteris paribus* assumption). Any changes in other markets may upset the calculations of consumers and/or producers and thus change the amount people want to buy and sell at each price. These adjustments will be reflected in shifts in either or both of the demand and supply curves. Consider for example the effect on the coffee market of a fall in tea prices resulting from a sudden glut of tea. If consumers regard tea and coffee as rival goods, a fall in the price of tea will encourage some consumers to switch from coffee to tea, with the result that at any given coffee price, less coffee will now be demanded. The effect is therefore to shift the demand curve for coffee to the left although there will be probably little effect on the supply curve for coffee since most producers will not be in a position to switch rapidly from tea to coffee production. Under the new demand conditions, we may expect the market-clearing price of coffee to rise to a new equilibrium level, say p^{**}, as is illustrated in figure 1.6. A change in cost conditions because of a change in labour costs is an example of an event that would result in a shift in the supply curve: a rise in wages may be expected to reduce the number of units produced at any given price level resulting in a leftward shift of the supply curve and a rise in the equilibrium price of the product. Whether this rise in wages has any effect on the demand for coffee will depend upon whether the workers who now enjoy higher wages begin to consume more coffee and whether they account for a significant proportion of coffee sales.

The basic demand and supply analysis just outlined may be applied to virtually any market: labour markets, credit markets and housing markets may all be fruitfully approached with such apparatus just as may more obvious cases of markets for consumer goods and services. Law and legal institutions are important in the discussion of market operations for a variety of reasons. There may be laws governing the process of exchange itself, the obligations upon owners of different sorts of goods or assets, the terms upon which ownership claims may be traded, the ease with which firms can reduce the size of their work-force and so on. It is therefore rather surprising that until recently, economics has largely ignored the legal structure in which markets are embedded and equally that legal discussion has not made more intensive use of ideas from economics.

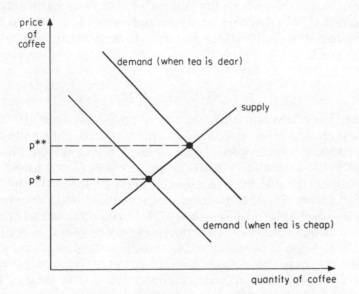

Figure 1.6 Response of Coffee Price to the Price of Tea

CONCLUDING REMARKS

The prospective contribution of economics is not limited to the analysis of market transactions. As should become clear in the course of this book, economic thinking and analysis can be applied in a great many instances where market transactions are not involved. Indeed some economists would argue that many legal institutions take the place of market transactions. It seems natural however to use the analysis of markets as a starting point. The demand and supply analysis introduced in this chapter may occupy a central position in economics, but it is not the only concern and in addition it has some much deeper implications and more subtle implications than may be apparent from the rather lightweight approach of the foregoing sections.

The principal object of this first chapter has been to introduce the *dramatis personae* and to set out the rudiments of demand and supply analysis and market behaviour. The next chapter examines the notion of cost, one of the basic elements of economic analysis and something that is of considerable significance, particularly in the context of legal discussion.

FURTHER READING

The basic elements of microeconomics outlined in this chapter are investigated much more thoroughly in most introductory textbooks of economics: see for example Lipsey (1979) or Lancaster (1974). A more rigorous treatment of consumer choice that anticipates some of the problems of aggregating across consumers, discussed further in chapter 3 below, is chapter 1 of Winch (1971). Further discussion of the historical development of economics may be found in Barber (1967). A more advanced treatment of consumers, firms and markets may be found in Layard and Walters (1978), although this is not recommended for the beginner. An introduction to the application of economic reasoning to the law is to be found in the opening two chapters of Posner's classic text, Posner (1977). The reader who has studied economics at an introductory level only may find it useful to consult an intermediate text such as Hirshleifer (1976) or Asimakopulos (1978).

2

Costs

INTRODUCTION

In the latter part of the previous chapter it was suggested that price served the pre-eminent role of ensuring the adjustment of demand and supply until they were in balance. The present chapter takes a closer look at the notion of price and its relation to the more general notion of a cost. As the reader may already suspect the two words are not interchangeable. An understanding of the differences and similarities between the two concepts and of how one makes the transition from one to the other is of central importance in the application of economic thinking to legal problems.

Generally speaking, the cost of a resource is to be thought of as representing the value of the most attractive alternative use to which it could be put. When a consumer buys a car for example, the cost he incurs is essentially that he will have to surrender some part of his wealth in exchange for the car, wealth which he will thus not be able to use for buying anything else. The presumption is that the decision to buy the car implies that the consumer puts a higher value upon the car than upon any other bundle of goods he could buy with the same amount of wealth. Whilst the 'cost' of buying a car is given by the opportunities that one thereby foregoes so the 'cost' of taking a job will be the loss of leisure time and energy that the worker could otherwise have used in enjoyable pursuits or in some other job open to him.

The notion of cost may now be compared with the notion of price. Price represents the terms on which goods and services may be bought on the market, whilst cost represents

21

the sacrifice of alternative goods and services embodied in a good or service. The two may differ quite radically. This is probably best illustrated by Milton Friedman's assertion that there is no such thing as a 'free lunch'. If my publisher takes me out to lunch to talk business and pays the bill, I pay a price of zero for my meal. The important point however is that whilst the lunch has been free to me it has nevertheless generated a cost and this cost has to be met by someone. The identity of the final payer may be quite difficult to determine: if publishers are accustomed to dining authors, such costs will be spread amongst authors themselves (whose royalties will be lower than if such customs were not followed), amongst the book-buying public (who will be charged a higher price for books than they would be otherwise) and amongst publishers (who will make lower profits than they might expect if they avoided such actions). All costs have to be met by someone, but not necessarily by the user of a good or service. Taxes and subsidies, for example constitute a device that may be used to drive a wedge between price and cost although they are not the only one. The provision of public services such as health and education generates costs which are borne for the most part by the taxpayer rather than by the users of such services. The nationalised industries generally receive subsidies in one form or another from the government (and thus the taxpayer) so that whilst buyers of goods from nationalised industries pay a price for the goods, this price will often be lower than the relevant cost of producing the goods.

Just as buyers of goods, or consumers, may be subsidised and pay a price that is lower than cost so too they sometimes generate costs themselves that are met by others. If, for example, I buy a hi-fi set that I play very loudly, I may be imposing costs on my neighbours. That is to say that whilst I may have paid a market price that reflects the full cost of producing the equipment, I may subsequently use it in such a way as to destroy the tranquillity of the neighbour-hood. Such destruction represents a genuine cost, provided that my neighbours are peace-lovers because quiet, which is a scarce resource, is being used up in the course of my consumption of the good in just the same way as various components, materials and labour time were used up initially in the construction of the hi-fi set. Thus whilst costs may at their simplest refer to the value of the goods and services used in the production of a commodity, they may also arise when people use goods in particular ways. Further, there may be instances in which individuals may generate costs without using any goods or services at all. Violent behaviour for example may cause distress to victims or potential victims, such distress representing a cost to the extent that the victims would be prepared to pay for (because they would value) its prevention.

Before looking at some more particular categories of costs, it might be well to comment upon a popular misconception about cost. Consider the following claim: 'The house no longer costs us anything because we finished paying off the mortgage last year.' The reader should be able to detect that this argument is nonsense if one interprets costs, as we have urged, to reflect the opportunities foregone. The cost of having one's wealth tied up in the form of a house is that one is missing the opportunity of holding the same volume of wealth in the form of other assets like works of art or whatever or of converting the wealth into cash and spending the proceeds on everyday goods and services. For many people the opportunity cost of owning a house is quite high being measured by the market price of the house. It should be remembered however that people have to live somewhere so that the relevant choice for the home owner is between, inter alia, (i) selling the house, buying a cheaper one and spending the difference on non-house items, (ii) selling the house and renting somewhere to live and (iii) keeping the house. The choice that the individual makes between these alternatives will reflect, amongst other things, the individual's inclination to accumulate assets, the individual's attitudes towards his heirs, the state of the rental sector of the housing market and so forth. The calculation of opportunity cost may thus be quite a complex one.

SOCIAL AND PRIVATE COST

One useful way of distinguishing between some of the different categories of cost identified in the previous section is to use the terms social and private cost. Social cost refers to the total cost involved in producing a good or service or in pursuing some particular course of action. Private cost refers to that part of total cost which it falls to the individual to meet. To take a standard example, a factory producing chemicals that discharges effluent into a nearby stream will be generating costs of various kinds. Basic production costs such as the buying of raw materials, the rent of land and the hiring of labour will be met, in full, by the firm. It may be however, that the pollution of the stream which occurs as a by-product will generate costs that the firm does not have to meet. Reduced fishing catches and the destruction of leisure amenities resulting from the pollution will impose costs on residents downstream, but these may be costs that the firm can avoid having to pay. In this instance, the social cost of production (which will include the losses from pollution) will exceed the private cost that the firm incurs.

The important consequence of there being a divergence between private cost and social cost is that an 'inefficient' pattern of production will emerge. In order to justify and explain this remark, we begin by recalling the demand and supply apparatus of the previous chapter. The demand for a product depends upon its market price: those consumers choosing to buy a product priced at p_1 must value it at p_1 or more. The supply of a product on the other hand depends upon the cost of production: as the cost of producing the last unit of output rises, firms will produce less (if market price is to remain unaltered) or will set a higher price or both. In choosing its production level or price, the polluting firm will be influenced by the extent to which it has to meet the costs of pollution. If this private cost should be significantly less than social cost, that is if the firm can avoid paying for a major part of pollution costs, then the firm will be producing 'too much'. For production to be efficient we require that the value of a good being produced be at least as great as the costs incurred in its production. This comparison should of course be based on social rather than private cost since we are considering the overall picture and whether resources are best used in one part of the economy or another. The relevant condition for efficiency is thus whether the value of the product exceeds its social cost, whereas the firm considers only whether the product's value exceeds its private cost.

A geometrical version of this argument appears as figure 2.1. Demand for the product is given by D whilst two supply curves appear. S_1 sets out the amounts that manufacturers will be prepared to produce at different price levels if they can avoid paying pollution costs. The second supply curve S_2 traces out the amounts that will be produced at different prices if producers are forced to meet pollution costs in full. At any given price level, polluters who have to pay will offer less units for sale than will firms in otherwise similar circumstances who are exempt from paying pollution costs.

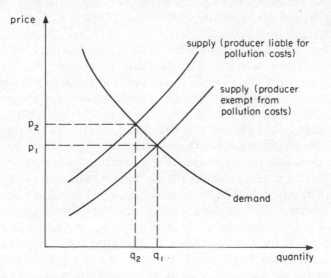

Figure 2.1 Overproduction by Firms Exempt from Pollution Costs

As may be seen from the diagram, the outcome will be that in equilibrium, if firms are exempt they will supply an amount q_1 and the market price will be p_1, whilst if firms are not exempt they will produce less (q_2) and a higher market price (p_2) will emerge.

CORRECTING DIVERGENCES BETWEEN SOCIAL AND PRIVATE COST

The traditional remedy advanced by economists for divergences of this kind between social and private costs was the use of corrective taxes. Following the work of the English economist Pigou earlier this century, it seemed that the best solution was to impose a tax on each unit of output of the polluting firm equal in size to the damage being generated. Suppose, for example, that each unit of output generated the same amount of damaging effluent and that this amount caused harm measured in financial terms of h. If the government were to impose a tax of h on each unit that the firm produced, in the form, let us say, of a sales tax, then producers might be induced to behave in just the same way as they would when paying directly for pollution. An important paper published by Ronald Coase in 1961 triggered off a major change in the attitude taken by economists towards the tax solution advocated by Pigou. Coase argued that the institution of legal liability was able, at least in principle, to bring about precisely the same outcome as the Pigovian tax. The potential advantage of using a system of legal liability rather than the tax system was that it was no longer necessary for the government to try and calculate the size of h, that is the cost of the damage being caused, since the parties involved could make their own judgments and act accordingly. Legal liability could thus be regarded as a device by which apparent divergences between social and private costs (or *externalities* as these divergences are called) could be eliminated by what amounts to enabling the affected parties to bargain amongst themselves. Instead of a person suffering from the damage being caused by a polluter having to rely upon the government to intervene, via the tax system or via the imposition of a statutory prohibition of the activity in question, on their behalf they could now take direct action in the form of a civil law action. In his paper, which is long and rather difficult, Coase examines in detail a long series of cases brought under English law and demonstrates that they represent a sophisticated means of dealing with the problem of social cost.

Before looking at what has come to be known as the Coase Theorem in more depth it is well to point out that the institution of legal liability has drawbacks as well as advantages. Principal amongst these disadvantages is the problem of transactions costs. In order for civil law remedies to be an effective means of controlling externalities, it is vital that the civil law can be used cheaply. If the negotiation and bargaining that is to take place under a set of liability rules should itself be costly then it may be that the imposition of more or less arbitrary solutions by government is to be preferred. What then are the costs of operating a system of private rights? In essence, these costs are the costs of transacting: that is to say the costs of retaining legal advisers, the costs of the act of bargaining itself which may be acrimonious and unpleasant and so forth. Imposing government solutions is of course not costless: tax collectors will be needed if a tax solution is imposed and inspectors will be needed if a system of prohibition is used. In either case, decisions will have to be made about the design of the regulations and about the size of penalties and so on. In the case of private transactions however, costs will be more to do with the activities of preparing and prosecuting private legal actions. If a factory is discharging effluent, there may be very many single individuals who are incurring harm as a result, and equally, each individual may be suffering harm that is the result of the activities of more than one firm. This will mean that, unless actions are instituted allowing those affected to band together and pursue the matter as a single case, the costs of taking any legal action are likely to become prohibitive for the individual. Difficulties of proving which firm (or firms) is responsible may raise the costs of pursuing legal action beyond the level of the benefits that may be expected. For some commentators these difficulties are seen to be a pervasive drawback of using a private system of negotiation whilst for others such difficulties are seen as less troublesome than the task of ensuring that any government intervention be socially beneficial.

Returning to the Coase Theorem itself, it is a most noteworthy feature that the Theorem incorporates the proposition that it does not matter which way liability is assigned initially. Provided that transactions costs can be ignored, the parties will always bargain themselves into the same position. This proposition is crucial because it implies that whilst it is important that there be liability rules of some kind, it does not really matter what form they take. A classic example is that of the railroad and the farmer. The railroad, along which run trains that emit sparks, crosses the land of a farmer. The farmer grows corn, but frequently loses his crop from fires caused by sparks from the locomotives. The question is, how should liability for the damage caused be allocated in this case?

Suppose first that we impose liability for any damage on the farmer himself. The farmer can if he wishes offer money to the railway company either to reduce or eliminate completely, use of the railroad. Alternatively the farmer may compensate the railway for introducing damage-reducing moves, such as spark guards or driving trains at a lower speed, if this would reduce fire risks. At the same time of course the farmer can implement schemes himself to reduce fire losses: by planting further away from the railway line or planting a different variety of corn that is more fire-resistant he may be able to reduce his losses. The important point is that the farmer will take a variety of steps to try and raise his profits but will only be prepared to pay compensation or increase his own costs up to the point where his last pound of expenditure on fire prevention yields an increase in revenue (as a result of higher production) of one pound.

Suppose now that we reverse the argument and impose liability upon the railway company. The same sorts of preventive measures will be considered by the railway company, provided that we assume that it is a profit-maximizer and provided also that we retain our assumption of zero transactions costs. The installation of spark guards or the slowing down of trains will be considered, as will moves to offer the farmer compensation for moving his crop further away from the path of the railroad. The argument is perfectly symmetrical, and the railroad will pursue all of those moves which generate lower fire losses than they cost to implement and reject all of those that are not 'profitable'. Thus whichever way liability is allocated, the same set of fire prevention activities will be adopted and the same level of output will be chosen by both parties.

It should be noted that in the event that damage costs and prevention costs are both very high, either assignment of liability may result in the activity being discontinued. If the railroad is liable, it will choose not to run any trains if there is no package of preventive activities that can be implemented that will generate revenue that exceeds costs. That is to say that the railroad will find that its profits from running the service will be less than the amount of compensation it has to pay the farmer. Similarly, if the farmer is made liable, he will find it cheaper to compensate the railway company for withdrawing the service than to suffer fire losses. Thus we may conclude *either assignment of liability will ensure that resources are used in the most valuable possible way,* for in either case, pursuit of profit will enable only those activities and those precautions which offer revenue in excess of costs to be pursued.

This finding, it must be stressed, is only true when the parties involved can bargain costlessly. It seems natural to ask whether this assumption of zero transactions costs is sensible, or whether it is wise to push the analysis further and to discover what may be said about the optimal method for assigning liability in instances where transactions costs *are* significant.

TRANSACTIONS COSTS

A closer look at the notion of transactions costs reveals that they come in many different forms and that in some contexts they are likely to be much greater than others. It can further be shown that taking explicit account of transactions costs, one can generate rules for deciding upon the allocation of liability. The question of what assignment of liability affords consumers the best degree of protection represents a good example of an area in which there is controversy about transactions costs. It is possible to take the view that consumers themselves should take responsibility for damage that they incur as a result of the failure of a product that they have bought. It is equally possible to argue that producers should be liable (whether strictly or otherwise) for damage caused by use of their products. The choice between these alternatives (the choice between the doctrines of *caveat emptor* and *caveat venditor*) may be regarded as a non-issue if one adopts the assumption of the Coase theorem and supposes that either group could costlessly implement their rights. If, as seems likely, one chooses to reject this assumption as unrealistic and misleading, then a real issue arises, and it will become important to investigate the substance of the transactions costs that arise.

Nearly all goods that are traded are potentially harmful in some way, but equally, are beneficial in many other ways. Some goods are of course more likely to cause harm than others, and the amount of damage potential is much greater in some cases than others. Medical equipment and the ropes used by mountaineers are products upon which peoples' lives will depend in a very direct way: defects in either may have very serious consequences. Egg cups and fountain pens on the other hand are much less likely to cause harm if they are defective in some way, although they may still be potentially poisonous or otherwise harmful. Transactions costs do not of course depend upon the extent of these potential damage costs. Rather, the relevant transactions costs are those associated with the actions of buyers and sellers of the product. If consumers do not have an enforceable right against a manufacturer, they may be expected to exercise more care in choosing between different available products. They may also exercise greater care when using the product and may also find it expedient to take out private insurance to guard against the possible consequences of injury from using a product. The sellers, or manufacturers, of the product may by contrast be confronted with liability for damage caused to consumers. Such an assignment of liability would call forth a set of actions that differ from those where consumers are made liable. Manufacturers may find it profitable to be more careful about the quality of goods that they sell. They will probably also find themselves involved in legal actions brought by consumers, and will accordingly hire legal resources to combat such actions and take out insurance against the possibility of having to concede claims.

All of the activities that have just been described are costly: someone will have to foot the bill. In essence, the choice of liability rule can be thought of as being a choice between the benefits and costs associated with the alternatives, with the objective being to isolate the rule that offers the greatest net benefit. It can be shown that the best set of rules will be the one which exploits the likelihood that one side may be able to eliminate costs more cheaply than the other. The notion of least-cost avoidance will normally enable some conclusion to be drawn about the assignment of liability that will minimise aggregate costs.

In other contexts, particularly in the area of contract law, transactions costs may be a dominant influence not just on the desirability of particular kinds of rules, but on the whole economic environment. The high costs of negotiating contracts may give rise to pressure not just for contract law to take particular forms, but also for some transactions to be taken 'out of the marketplace' altogether and organised within firms. This has the important consequence that the substance of legal rules may have far wider implications than those which are apparent from an examination of the pattern of contracts which are actually agreed in everyday trading. Transactions costs are therefore themselves an important focus for work on the structure of economic and legal organisation.

CONCLUDING REMARKS

It has been shown in this chapter that there are several different categories into which costs may be put, and that in many cases a full appreciation of these different kinds of costs will be a prerequisite of well-informed discussion of almost any legal question. Reliance on this rather wide definition of costs is a feature of later chapters (chapter 4 onwards) in which we investigate very different kinds of legal question. In chapters 4 – 6, which are concerned with crime punishment and the administration of justice, it is shown that the various activities involved (from the decisions being made by the prospective criminal to the decisions being made about how much to spend on pursuing offenders who fail to pay fines imposed on them by the courts) all entail various kinds of costs. By identifying what these costs are and where they fall, it is possible to derive conclusions about how the criminal justice system might be looked at from an efficiency standpoint. In the section on civil law which follows the criminal section, it is shown that tort and contract are both areas in which cost considerations play a most important role. The remaining chapters perhaps to a lesser extent, illustrate that the extent and pattern of use of the law by citizens will reflect cost factors.

In the next chapter, which concludes our introduction to economics, we move from the notion of cost to issues of valuation and evaluation. Valuation is a matter that lies at the heart of an understanding of a great number of decisions and choices being made by economic agents. Evaluation on the other hand is the main issue when it comes to the broader decisions and choices that have to be made by society at large or on its behalf. Common to both issues is the question of how costs may be measured in 'difficult' areas. Thus whilst the discussion of costs in the present chapter can sometimes be applied directly, it will often be found that some of the hazards discussed in the next chapter have to be overcome first.

FURTHER READING

The analysis of this chapter is more specialised than that which appears in chapter 1. The reader is best advised to look at an intermediate text such as Hirshleifer (1976) rather than an introductory text. For a further discussion of externalities see Culyer (1973) and on the correction of the divergence between private and social cost see chapter 6 of Layard and Walters (1978). The classic source on the nature of social cost is Coase (1960). A useful discussion of transactions costs, particularly in the context of contract, is Williamson (1979, 1981).

3

Valuation and Evaluation

In the previous two chapters we have outlined, albeit briefly, the way in which economists approach behaviour and the very important notion of cost. This chapter is devoted principally to methods of appraisal, but draws heavily upon the two earlier chapters. The object of addressing the question of appraisal is mainly to show that economic theory can be used to develop methods of valuing a great variety of gains and losses, but also to show that economic methods can be and are often misused.

In the course of this chapter we begin by looking at the problem of how economists calculate the value of an asset and at some of the difficulties they are likely to encounter in doing so. We move then to consider the question of how one is to proceed when a variety of assets is at stake and in particular to the problem of evaluating legal policy or legal institutions in circumstances where some individuals stand to make gains whilst others stand to make losses. It is clear that a bundle of techniques or rules that enable one to place a value on a single gain or loss may not be sufficiently powerful to enable evaluation of controversial policies, but we will argue that they represent a very useful starting point.

BASIC PRINCIPLES OF VALUATION

It should be emphasised from the start that economists do not always value things in the same way as actuaries (whose job is

34

mainly to calculate the appropriate size of premia in private insurance markets) or professional valuers (whose job is to predict the price that a *particular* asset will realise when marketed) or accountants (whose job is to compile accurate financial records of what has already happened). Although economists will often be interested in the figures thrown up in the course of market transactions, they are often interested also in inferring costs and values in contexts where market valuations cannot be directly used. This concern may of course be shared with others, including many solicitors, barristers and judges. Civil law is perhaps the obvious area in which calculations of losses, damages and costs commonly take place but, as will be illustrated in later chapters, cost assessment may play an important role in decision-making in the criminal justice system and in the design and implementation of regulatory policy.

The basic object of valuation is to find a financial sum that expresses in terms of today's values the future benefits that an asset represents. A (non-indexed) government security offers a fixed nominal income in each year until it matures and will then repay a fixed nominal sum. There is no real problem in valuing such an asset because there are large numbers of such securities in existence, there are well-developed markets on which they may be traded and there is no ambiguity about the income-earning capacity of such bonds. To establish the value of a particular security of this kind, one simply looks at the appropriate place in the financial section of the newspaper.

Exactly the same object characterises the attempt to establish the value of a tort claim. A man has been injured in an accident caused by the negligence of a third party: his earning prospects are impaired, his hearing is impaired and his irreplaceable antique car ruined beyond repair. What value are we to assign to his loss? There seem to be three quite different sorts of assets involved, but it is not clear on the surface whether the same sorts of methods could be applied in valuing each of them. As far as an economist is concerned, it should be possible to find a way of expressing all types of loss as a fixed sum of money, although the methods for estimating the sum may be different for the different components of cost.

The problem of valuation also confronts the trader who knows that he can sell his goods for one price today but is offered a contract under which he stands to receive a higher price at some time in the future. How is he to compare an offer of £110 receivable in 12 months' time with an offer of £100 today? In order to illustrate the solution of this problem, and as a prelude to investigating the more complex problem of the injured man's losses we begin by looking at discounting.

Discounting

Let us suppose that a government bond was issued some time ago with a face value of £100, that it offers a nominal interest rate of 15 per cent per annum, that it is redeemable in five years' time and that the current rate of interest is 10 per cent. The value that we may expect this bond to exhibit today is measured by the current price that would ensure that this bond offered the same yield as other financial instruments currently available. In order to calculate this yield it is important to remember that it is worth less to receive £100 next year or in 1990 than it is to receive the same sum today. If we receive the £100 today we could invest it in a building society at, say, 13 per cent so that one year hence the account would contain £113 (or rather more if receipts of interest are added back in the meanwhile). Expressed the other way round, we would only have to invest £88.50 today in order to ensure that the account stood at £100 in one year's time. Considerably less (namely £29.46) would have to be invested today if the £100 target did not have to be reached for ten years. Thus it is that the further in the future that a payment is due to be received, the lower the equivalent amount to which immediate receipt would correspond. More technically, it is necessary to discount future receipts (and outgoings) by a factor that takes account of the fact that the sum cannot be earning interest in the interim. If we assume that the appropriate rate for discounting is given by the current rate of interest, then sums receivable in one year should be multiplied by $1/(1 + r)$ to calculate their present value whilst sums receivable in two years should be multiplied by $1/(1 + r)^2$ and so on, so that in general, receipts in t years time should be multiplied by $1/(1 + r)^t$. When using this formula, r should be expressed as 0.1 if interest rates are 10 per cent p.a., as 0.2 if they are 20 per cent and so forth.

Throughout this section we use a slightly oversimplified method of calculation. Although we are applying compound rather than simple interest rates, we assume that the compounding is done annually rather than continuously. This simplifies the algebra but slightly overstates net project value. For an outline of the more sophisticated method see a specialist text such as Chiang (1974) or Sugden and Williams (1978).

Using our simplified method, the present value (PV) of £100 receivable in two years, if the discount rate is 10 per cent, may be calculated as:

$$PV = 100/(1 + 0.1)^2 = 82.6$$

Using the same approach, the present value of the government security is calculated by discounting the receipts of income from the bond and adding the discounted value of the bond at redemption. In total therefore we get:

$$PV = \frac{15}{(1 + 0.1)} + \frac{15}{(1 + 0.1)^2} + \frac{15}{(1 + 0.1)^3}$$

$$+ \frac{15}{(1 + 0.1)^4} + \frac{115}{(1 + 0.1)^5}$$

$$= 12.40 + 11.17 + 10.15 + 9.23 + 64.33$$

$$= 107.28$$

The first term on the right-hand side of the equation refers to the £15 interest to be received in twelve months' time, the

second term to the £15 interest to be received in two years'
time and so on. The final term refers to the interest plus the
principal which will be paid to the bond owner at redemption
in five years' time. One would expect the current market price
to reflect the present value of the security.

It can incidentally be seen easily at this point why there is a
negative relationship between interest rates and the value of
government bonds. As the market rate of interest rises, it is
only by reducing the price at which government securities can
be bought that their yield can be maintained. In the example
above, if market rates were to rise to 20 per cent the present
value of the bond would fall to £85.05. The intuitive reason
for this is that future receipts are now worth less in today's
terms, because a lower sum would have to be set aside today
to generate £15 in any future year. It is interesting also to
observe that this finding has the more general consequence
that the value of assets or wealth is inversely related to
prevailing interest rates: the higher the interest rate the less
valuable is the prospect of earning returns in future years.

Asset values, market price and speculation

All assets, be they financial assets like stocks and shares,
physical assets like land or cars or 'human' assets or
capacities, have a net present value. This value measures the
worth, properly discounted, of the services that the asset will
offer in the future. The value of the asset will generally be a
guess or forecast: no-one knows for sure what tomorrow will
bring, with the consequence that no-one can put a wholly
reliable figure on net present value. The market price of an
asset reflects the view that traders in the asset take of its
future prospects. Any events which influence traders' views
will influence asset values. This is most clearly seen in the
behaviour of stock markets where continually changing views
about the prospects of individual firms and of firms generally
are reflected in frequent adjustment of stock prices.

It should be stressed that price reflects all available
information about the future. In order for an asset's price to
change therefore there has to be some change in what people
believe will happen in the future. Changes of this kind can be

triggered by all sorts of external events but also by changes in the sentiments of the most active traders. When announcements are made about changes in government policy that have not been fully anticipated, for example, asset prices will experience a once-for-all change as the news is incorporated into calculations of net present value. This is just the same as an equity share increasing in value upon an announcement that the annual dividend is to be greater than had been assumed by the stock market.

The role of speculation deserves a mention at this point. If some traders think that they 'know better than the market' about an asset's future earning power, they may speculate in the asset. Particularly if they think that the asset is underpriced, that is that its net present value exceeds the existing market price, then they will start buying the asset in question − quite possibly on borrowed money. If and when the market comes round to a similar view the speculator will make gains because the increasing pressure to buy the asset will force its market price upward. The speculator, once he thinks that market price has reached its peak, will then sell the asset and record a windfall gain. Speculators can of course lose, but it can be shown that since speculation is probably *on average* profitable (since otherwise people would not be tempted to speculate) markets are more stable than they would otherwise be. That is to say that markets are a very efficient mechanism for transmitting views about future prospects, and that speculation has the effect of speeding up the rate at which new information, or better-informed guesses, can be absorbed.

Speculation is not an unqualified good however. The prospects of making short-term gains may make it potentially worthwhile for traders to seek inside information. Previews of company results and advance knowledge of government activities may be potentially very profitable, and it is quite likely that resources will be used in the search for such 'superior' information. From a social point of view such activities are wasteful: they absorb rather than generate resources. That is not to say that speculation is undesirable but rather that it may have some unattractive side effects.

Having argued that net present value calculations will have a vital effect on the market price of assets, it should be noted that there are some circumstances in which such calculations are important even where there is no intention to trade in the subject matter of the calculation. When a firm signs a contract to supply a commodity for example, it can calculate the net present value of the deal. By comparing the present value of the revenue that the firm expects to receive with the present value of the costs of production, the firm can establish how profitable the venture promises to be. Similarly, as we now show, the basic method of valuation can be applied in efforts to calculate the present value of the losses that a victim of tort has incurred.

Valuing income loss

Let us suppose that at the time of an accident a man's income was £10,000 p.a. and that he was expecting it to rise by 10 per cent p.a. until his retirement five years' hence. Ignoring any effect on his pension, let us suppose that the effect of the accident was to reduce his prospects by a half and let us also suppose that the relevant interest rate is 8 per cent. There are two closely-related ways in which the loss could be calculated. The first, which is slightly cumbersome, is to calculate the present value of earnings just before the accident and to measure the loss as the difference between this figure and the present value of earnings recalculated following the accident. The second, neater way is to discount the change in earnings in each future year and to express this sum as a present value. On the assumption that the salary would be paid in arrears at the end of each year, the second method of calculation gives:

$$PV_{loss} = 5,000/1.08 + 5,500/1.08^2 + 6,050/1.08^3$$
$$+ \ 6,655/1.08^4 + 7,321/1.08^5$$
$$= 4,630 + 4,715 + 4,803 + 4,892 + 4,983$$
$$= 24,023$$

This procedure for valuing gains and losses, income

streams or whatever contains no reference to 'multipliers' or 'multiplicands'. The methods used by judges for calculating compensation awards in cases of personal injury have however been discussed at length and criticised elsewhere. The interested reader may pursue these matters by looking at a text on tort such as Ogus (1973), Chapter 6(e) and comparing the 'legal' method with the 'economic' method as outlined here and elsewhere. The next concern is to look at some of the difficulties that the present value method, or any other method for that matter, may encounter. Although we have calculated a measure of the loss of earnings for the man with the tort claim, it is not obvious how we may apply the formula to his loss of hearing or to his loss of an irreplaceable car.

Valuing Life and Limb

It is useful, if sometimes distasteful, to be able to apply money sums to losses that involve human suffering and loss of life. Government Departments, for example, confront choices between spending more on kidney machines or more on heart transplants, but not both: they confront choices between improving roads in the hope of eliminating accident blackspots or building more motorways to speed up traffic flows and so on. In confronting choices of this kind values will be placed on human life and limb whether government recognises the fact or not. Decisions can only be made if values are assigned implicitly or explicitly to unpleasant outcomes. In many areas of civil law, provision is made for those incurring injuries to recover compensation from parties from whose negligence the injuries may be judged to result. Injuries may be painful at the time and may cause lasting effects in the form of chronic pain or disability. Measures of lost income will not account for such losses, but that is not to say that the injuries are any less real.

There is no single answer to the question of how life and limb is to be valued, and it is not surprising that the value of life used in different agencies should vary so much. An approach advocated by some economists, the implicit subjective valuation approach as one may term it, relies on the argument that individuals frequently have to make choices in which their own safety is at stake, and that it may be possible to learn something about the values that individuals put on their own lives by studying such choices. Decisions about the speed at which to drive along motorways, about whether to fly with the cheap airline with a poor safety record, or about whether to buy more expensive car tyres with better grip are all decisions which, at least implicitly, require value to be put on human life. The argument runs that if the individual can be taken to have knowledge of the change in the probability of death or serious injury associated with switching from one option to another, this change in probability can be compared with the price at which the individual is prepared to switch. We can imagine the consumer being prepared to switch to the less safe airline provided that it is cheaper by a sufficient amount than the other airline. A value can therefore be assigned to a change in the probability of death or injury, and by making certain assumptions it is possible to translate the size of the sum needed to induce greater exposure to risk into a value for life and limb. The work that has been done in this area, principally by Jones-Lee (1976) suggests that the subjective values that individuals assign to greater safety exceed the figures used by the Department of the Environment, and other agencies who use such figures, by a very considerable margin. The difficulty of course is that these figures are subjective, and may vary widely from person to person. Road and hospital builders on the other hand will generally be dealing with 'statistical lives': they will not know the identity of the individuals who stand to gain from the improvement of facilities. In the context of civil law, the problem is likely to be that it is difficult to get a victim, or party who has incurred harm, to answer reliably questions of the form: 'how much loss has this injury caused you?'

The two areas looked at so far have really been polar cases: income losses can be readily assessed by reference to market prices whilst losses of life and limb are rather difficult to measure. Between these two extremes lies a very large grey area in which greater or lesser degrees of difficulty arise. We will restrict ourselves to a very brief treatment of some of them.

Valuing Leisure and Property

For some purposes it is useful to be able to assign a value to leisure time: if events or policies should raise or lower the amount of leisure time (by reducing commuter time for example) it will be useful to have a value for such time so that it can be made commensurable with other categories of costs and benefits. The normal argument here is that provided that only a small degree of variation is involved, the wage rate can be used as a proxy measure. The grounds for this argument lie in the notion of opportunity cost. When workers are making decisions about how many hours to work, about whether to do overtime or even about whether to enter occupations that are known to entail longer working hours they are implicitly trading greater income prospects against more leisure time. It can be argued as a result that for the last hour of work and for the first hour of leisure the worker is somewhere near the margin at which the value of income received lies close to the value of leisure time. This approximate equality at the margin can be exploited by making the claim that the level of income received for the last hour of work will be quite a good proxy measure for the value of leisure that is foregone when this hour is worked. Thus if for example we find workers turning down the opportunity to work overtime at rates that are much higher than basic pay, we may conclude that the hours of leisure time are highly-prized by the worker. Conversely, the currently unemployed may be very happy to sacrifice part of their plentiful leisure time in return for a modestly-paid job (ignoring any complications about entitlement to benefit and so on).

The value of many forms of property damage or loss may be inferred from markets in a fairly direct way. The damage to a car can be estimated by comparing the amount for which the damaged car could be sold and the amount which one would have to pay to secure a car that is similar in all germane respects to the car before it was damaged. Such calculations are done frequently by insurance companies, and in most instances it will be very easy to gather the appropriate information. In the case of an 'irreplaceable' antique car, matters may be more difficult: the insured value may understate the value of the car to the owner, and almost by definition there will not exist a market in cars of that particular kind. Nevertheless, unless the car is completely and utterly wrecked, restoration will generally be feasible: it does not matter in principle that it might be extremely costly. Equally, it will generally be possible to estimate the amount that the car would have fetched before the accident because one could examine the price that such cars have fetched in the past and one could examine the prices that antique cars of a similar kind had recently fetched at auction. It should of course be pointed out that the market price will generally be lower than the subjective valuation of the car's owner because in keeping the car as long as he has the car owner is implying that he prefers to keep the car than to sell it. Nevertheless, by applying these arguments it is certainly possible to establish a lower bound on the asset's value. To give another example, it will generally be possible to establish the value that householders place on noise by investigating the change in property values that follows the construction of an airport or whatever in an area. People buying houses will, other things being equal, pay less for a noisy house than a quiet one, and by comparing appropriate properties it should be possible to derive some idea of the average value people put on quiet. An alternative procedure in the case of noise would be to investigate whether residents responded to construction of an airport by buying double-glazing or not. This would be another way of establishing the lowest value people put on noise, although this calculation may be misleading to the extent that although double glazing may reduce noise to previous levels in winter, it may in summer prevent the occupants from enjoying open windows and thus may rather underestimate damage. The lesson however seems clear enough: with some ingenuity it is possible to use market prices as surrogates for value in a wide variety of circumstances.

Risk and Uncertainty

Before considering how methods of valuing single items or assets may be utilised in developing methods of evaluating complicated policies affecting many different individuals, we look briefly at the way in which risk and uncertainty may be incorporated in measures of value. To take a very simple example, suppose that we were unsure about whether the man with the tort claim would have been promoted to foreman had he not had his accident. It seems likely that such a factor would be relevant since it would affect the amount of expected earnings and thus the present value of lost income.

There are two separable components of the problem of valuation under uncertainty: the first is to find a way of assigning probabilities and values to the various possible outcomes, whilst the second is to find a way of assessing the discount or premium that should be added to deal with the existence of uncertainty. Whilst the first of these propositions is fairly obvious the second is less so. To illustrate, consider the person (A) who is asked whether he would like to join a game. The rules of the game are that the person running the game (B) tosses a coin: if it lands heads, B pays A £1 and if it lands tails, A pays B £1. Assuming that the coin is unbiased and that B is a gentleman and will honour his debts, we may nevertheless be quite unsurprised if A should decline the opportunity to play the game. Thus even though the odds are even and payoffs of the two outcomes are symmetrical A may prefer to retain his existing wealth for certain than open himself to an even chance of becoming one pound richer or one pound poorer. We could of course extend the experiment in an attempt to establish how much we would have to pay A to induce him to agree to play: it might be a great deal. It is probably safe to assume that relatively few people are so enthusiastic about such games that they would be prepared to pay an entry fee to get into the game, for otherwise one would expect a great deal more gambling to be going on than one actually observes. Returning to the reticent player A, we may now offer him a different gamble. He is offered a choice between keeping his current job which pays £10,000 p.a. and a new job that pays £7,000 p.a. with a probability of 0.5 and £14,000 p.a. with the same probability. Will he take the new job? The expected salary in the new job may be calculated by weighting each outcome by its probability and adding across outcomes. The new job thus offers an expected salary of £10,500 p.a. which exceeds the salary in his old job, known for sure to be £10,000. Player A decides however that he will continue in his present job because he prefers the prospect of a certain income to the new proposition by more than £500.

Economists generally argue that a majority of people are *averse to risk,* that is that they will consistently turn down offers to gamble on absolutely fair terms and only accept uncertain prospects if they are offered compensation of some kind. The corollary of this is that most people will assign a rather lower value to an expected future income that is not known for sure than to a guaranteed income with the same expected value. It is possible to establish an individual's attitude towards risk either by direct experimentation or by inferring things from his responses to prevailing market opportunities. Either way it does seem clear that different individuals vary in the view that they take of risk, and that these differences may have some important implications for the way people behave in many everyday situations as well as in the rather contrived world of economists' examples.

The analysis thus far sketched out gives some idea of the reasonably sophisticated methods that can be applied in calculating individual values. These methods, as will become clear in later chapters, have a number of fairly direct applications in legal areas. For the moment, however, we turn our attention to the problems that arise when we attempt to aggregate gains and losses across individuals. The analysis and evaluation of many legal institutions demands that we have some systematic way of weighing up gains and losses. It is one thing to assess the losses that an individual has incurred: it is quite another to assess whether the rules of tort law taken as a whole, for example, produce better results than those which could be obtained by using different machinery.

MEASURING AGGREGATE GAINS AND LOSSES

It probably comes as no surprise to learn that the most widely-used method for calculating aggregate gains and losses is *Cost-Benefit Analysis,* CBA hereafter. Considerable publicity has been given at different times to a number of cost-benefit studies, particularly those which have concerned large prospective investment plans on the part of public authorities.

The essence of CBA is a comparison of all the costs and benefits associated with a policy change, where all cost and benefit streams are discounted to generate present values as outlined in the earlier part of this chapter. If the benefits, calculated in this way, should exceed the costs, there are *prima facie,* though not necessarily compelling, grounds for proceeding with the policy. It is important at the outset to note that the appropriate comparison is between what happens if the policy is pursued and what happens if it is rejected. In other words it is essential to have some way of predicting not only what will happen if we go ahead with the policy but also what will happen if we do not. The benefits to prospective passengers of increasing airport capacity for example will depend upon the extent to which existing facilities would become further congested if extra provision were not made, that is to say, that the benefit is measured by the difference between the speed and comfort of transition through the airport if the new facilities are added and the speed and comfort that could be expected if expansion did not occur. The fact that there are long delays at present may not be terribly relevant therefore to an assessment of the desirability of improving facilities: it is the prospect of delays or otherwise in the future that is relevant.

To take an example more obviously relevant to a discussion of legal institutions, there has been considerable controversy over legislation in the nineteenth century that gave greater responsibility to employers for work accidents. It has been suggested that it is not sufficient to investigate whether safety records improved following the introduction of the more stringent rules. Rather, some assessment is needed of what would have happened to safety levels if the legislation had not been implemented to act as a base for comparing the outcome that the legislation actually produced. This is of course just like arguing that when compensation is being calculated in a tort claim, losses are measured by comparing the earnings' prognosis before and after the event which occasioned the harm.

The apparently innocuous step of adding together gains and losses implicit in the example of the previous paragraph is a more controversial step than one might imagine. Greater safety for workmen will mean greater costs for employers, costs which they may absorb partly in the way of reduced profits but which will fall partly also upon consumers of the product in the form of higher prices. The greater safety may of course also reduce the wage level in the industry. A CBA of such a policy change involves adding together the gains to some individuals to the losses of others. It may be that workmen in this industry are poorly paid and often badly injured, whilst the product might only be consumed by the rich. The question is whether this would influence us to reach a different verdict about whether to implement safety legislation from the one that we would reach if the relative incomes of workmen and consumers were reversed, as would be the case in many areas of professional sport and entertainment for example. To take a more provocative example, the Concorde project embarked upon by the British government conferred benefits upon those who benefit from being able to fly around the world more quickly than before (the rich air travellers) and upon workers in factories where the plane was built who enjoyed enhanced employment opportunities (the lucky workers) whilst it conferred heavy costs upon those responsible for financing the British end of the project (the tax payer). Even if the benefits had been anywhere near costs, would we have been concerned about the configuration of groups experiencing the costs and benefits?

The view of many economists is that questions of this kind, questions of the distribution of income and wealth, are essentially political ones. There is nothing in economics, they would argue, that enables the analyst to presume that a gain of £1 to Jack is of more or less significance than a loss of £1 to Jill. The consequence of this view is that it is valuable for the analyst to give an indication of the size of benefits and costs and where they will fall, but not really legitimate for him to pronounce that benefits exceed costs simply because adding all the present values together gives a positive sum rather than a negative one.

Other economists take a harder line and are prepared to make distributive judgments. The main difficulty that this poses is that there are many possible criteria that might be applied, with no one criterion being manifestly 'right' or 'wrong'. Amongst the better known criteria are the following:

(i) HICKS-KALDOR TEST

This is probably much the most widely-used criterion and is the one that is closest to the one applied by many of those who are unfamiliar with the technical controversy. The test relies upon the proposition that if those who gain from a policy change could at least potentially compensate the losers, then the policy change should be approved. If for example, improving airport facilities involves construction costs of £100 million and will reduce property values in the vicinity by £20 million, but will bestow benefits on air travellers of £125 million, then construction should proceed. It will very often be impractical to create devices that permit the gainers to actually compensate the losers and thus the test will be a hypothetical one, albeit one that will generally be able to produce a decision.

(ii) PARETO TEST

This was the conservative criterion that dominated much applied economics before the writings of Hicks and Kaldor (in the late 1930s) had persuasively argued the case in favour of a test built upon potential compensation. Under the Pareto test, a policy change is to be approved if and only if it makes at least one person in the economy better off but makes no-one worse off. The status quo tends to do rather well under this criterion, since there are relatively few policy proposals that have exclusively beneficial or neutral effects.

(iii) RAWLSIAN CRITERION

Following the work of the philosopher John Rawls published in 1971, there are some people who are prepared to argue that the appropriate test of a policy is to look first at its effects on the least well-off. Should these effects be deleterious, the policy is rejected, irrespective of the size of benefits that it may bestow upon the better-off.

(iv) DISTRIBUTIONAL WEIGHTS

This is really a variant on the Hicks-Kaldor test, and proposes that explicit weights be assigned to the gains and losses accruing to different groups. That is to say that changes in the income levels of the less well-off may for example be assigned more importance than changes in the income levels of the better-off. At different times it has been suggested that these weights be inferred from previous policy decisions (an approach which requires a degree of consistency in previous policy-making that some might think unlikely) or that decision-makers be confronted with having to assign their own weights in order to reach a measure of total gains and losses.

Whilst one might want to berate economists for being so feeble-hearted as to say 'we can't tell you which is the best policy until you give us some idea of your views about justice or equity or the distribution of income', it is important to remember that some presumption will have to be made before a view is taken, and that the more explicitly informed is this presumption the more confident one can be that 'good' policies are being adopted and 'bad' policies are being rejected. To urge caution in the use of CBA may be to discourage people from commissioning such studies, and the more pragmatic economist would probably take the view that a misinterpreted cost-benefit study would produce sounder policy than no study at all.

An interesting development in the area of CBA has been the greatly increased attention paid to the problem of valuation in circumstances where it is felt that market prices do not fully reflect the 'costs' or 'opportunities foregone' of using resources in certain ways. The existence of taxation and subsidisation, the use of intervention policies by government in markets that distort price (for example, deliberate manipulation of interest rates) are but two examples of cases where market prices may not adequately measure the variables that would be appropriate in a cost-benefit study. In such instances, the conceptually correct procedure is to calculate what are called 'shadow prices' which reflect the real costs of using resources more accurately than the market prices. The method of calculation of these prices will be dependent upon the nature of the distortion at issue, and may involve reference to the price at which a good is traded on world markets, or it may involve making adjustments to the price observed on domestic markets. In some cases, a domestic market in the product may not exist or the good may be rationed in some way by the public authorities, with the result that some way has to be found of estimating the kind of price level that one might expect to emerge if the commodity were traded freely. In any event, the use of these apparently artificial prices will produce measures of costs and benefits that differ from those derived from more direct procedures.

Despite some of these more difficult technical features, the basic notion of CBA remains straightforward. By assessing the costs and benefits to all those people influenced by a policy change and by expressing them all as a present value, that is as a number of pounds at today's prices, the two can be directly compared. If benefits exceed costs proceed, if not, do not implement the change.

In contrast to CBA, Cost Effectiveness analysis (CE) sets out with a more limited objective. In CE studies, the benefits are taken to be the same for a variety of possible measures and the aim is to establish which of the alternatives is cheapest to implement. A cost-effective policy in the terminology of the economist is thus the least costly means of achieving some specified goal. To take a rather oversimplified example, if a new law is to be introduced and there are various ways in which the law may be enforced, the cost-effective method of enforcement is the one that generates the lowest level of costs whilst achieving some specified level or quality of enforcement. This use of the term 'cost-effective' is quite different from the way it is used by non-economists.

CONCLUDING REMARKS

In this chapter we have exploited the notion of costs developed in the previous chapter in such a way as to enable estimates to be made of losses suffered by individuals or of gains and losses experienced by society at large. These methods can in principle be applied to a wide range of issues. Within a particular set of rules they enable us to assess damages or at least to establish losses, whilst at another level they enable assessments to be made of whether particular sorts of legal institutions or legal rules seem to be more or less conducive to the good of society.

It is of considerable importance, when thinking about the ways in which economic arguments can be brought to bear upon legal issues, to remember that there are these different levels at which questions can be asked. Economists tend if anything to be concerned with thinking about the world at a higher level of abstraction than lawyers, particularly practising lawyers. They will tend for example to ask questions not about the meaning or interpretation of particular cases or judgments, but about whether contract law, or some particular part of it, is conducive to an efficient allocation of risk, or whether the tort system is a superior method of dealing with accidents as compared with other methods. This emphasis of course reflects the concerns within the discipline of economics, and the policy questions that applied economists generally tackle. That this emphasis should differ from the one that characterises the discipline of law is not surprising. What *is* perhaps a little surprising is that if the economist is willing to invest some time in the enterprise, he can apply his professional toolkit to the concerns of lawyers, whether practising or academic.

Although economists have for some time been involved in monopoly (or anti-trust) cases, they have as yet had only limited impact in other areas, particularly that of contract. There are however many fields of law to which a more thorough understanding of economic arguments can make a significant contribution. For this to happen, it is necessary for the economist to try and orientate his work in directions that make it more accessible to the lawyer and for lawyers to treat sympathetically the halting steps being taken by economists.

The following chapters rely at different places on various of the arguments we have used and assembled in the opening three chapters. The choice of subject area is dictated partly by the work that has been done by economists in the past, although the chapter headings give some idea of the efforts we make to set out the discussion in a way which will be reasonably intelligible to those who have a law background. Inevitably, in many places we have to oversimplify grossly discussion of the law, the operation of the economy or the economic theory being applied. The remainder of the book should be seen as only the merest glimpse of the sorts of things that economists can say about law and legal institutions.

FURTHER READING

Again, the concerns of this chapter are not very fully covered in introductory texts. A good starting place for discounting is chapter 16B of Hirshleifer (1976). For an introduction to the application of discounting to real-world problems, see chapter 8 of Culyer (1973) or Sugden and Williams (1978). A useful review of work on the value of life is Mooney (1977), although for a more general discussion see the very accessible book by Glover (1977). The incorporation of uncertainty into valuation is discussed in Layard and Walters (1978), but considerably more simply by Sugden and Williams (1978). The problem of aggregating across consumers is central to welfare economics: see, for example, Winch (1971).

4

The Economics of Crime

Whilst many people might agree that economics can be fairly naturally applied to law as it relates to essentially commercial matters like contracts, they might be less readily convinced that economics can be applied to questions of crime and punishment. The notion of rationally-calculating individuals who apply the same sorts of logic to decisions about whether to commit crime, and what sorts of crime to commit, as firms do to production decisions is perhaps not very palatable. Nevertheless there is considerable evidence that approaches based upon the assumption that criminals are basically rational in an economic sense can generate useful findings. It is the object of this part of the book to explore some of the familiar issues in the area of crime and punishment with the help of some basic economics.

THE DECISION TO COMMIT CRIME

The usual starting point for economists, following the pioneering work of Becker (1968), is to investigate the decision being made by a prospective offender about whether to commit crime or not. Crime, whether it involves theft or apparently 'non-economic' actions like violence, is assumed to benefit the offender in some way. At the same time, those committing crime will almost invariably realise that they face some prospect of being caught and that they may subsequently be punished. A 'rational' prospective offender is someone who takes account of both the benefits and costs associated with committing crime, and reaches his decision about whether or not to go ahead by reference to both. If costs, for whatever reason, should exceed benefits then a crime is avoided.

It is one thing to characterise decisions to commit crime in this rather general way but quite another thing to draw inferences about what sort of crime is actually committed or about how society may find it expedient to deal with crime. The next step is to be more precise about how both the costs and the benefits associated with crime are calculated by the would-be offender, for until this is clearly established any discussion of sentencing or enforcement policy will be vacuous.

Benefits to the Criminal

Looking first at the benefits to be enjoyed from criminal activity, two main points need to be made. First, numerical values can, at least in principle, be assigned to benefits and secondly, the size of these benefits may differ from the degree of harm crimes impose upon the rest of society. In some cases the benefit to be derived from crime may be clear-cut. If a person steals £100 in cash from someone else, and feels little or no remorse, then he has benefited to the tune of £100. Compare this however with the case of a thief stealing a colour TV set that would cost £300 to replace. The value to the criminal of his haul is given by the amount for which he can sell it, an amount that may be quite low because of the hazards of 'recycling' stolen goods. If a vigorous police campaign is being directed at such thefts or if many other individuals are stealing and trying to sell TV sets, or if the criminal has poor relations with 'fences' who dispose of the sets then the price he gets may be very low. Equally, thefts of goods with high sentimental value to their owners may afford the criminal little gain but the victim great harm.

In a rather similar way a vandal may get relatively little pleasure from causing damage that is very expensive to rectify, as is probably the case for example, with the causing of damage to parked cars. This is not however to say that the vandal is deriving no pleasure at all from his activities, indeed he would be jolly foolish to run the risk of conviction for an action that he would rather not commit!

Putting a particular value on some such benefits may be very difficult, but will generally, at least in principle, be possible. The basic argument that an economist would apply is that the benefit that the individual stands to gain as a result of crime can be measured by establishing the amount that the offender, in a market-like setting, would have to be offered in order to persuade him against committing the crime. If the value on the black market of stolen TV's is £30, then the prospective thief could probably be induced to not commit the crime by an offer of, let us say, £20. In this case, the size of the bribe is lower than the amount that he would actually get if he stole the TV because he does not have the bother of actually committing the crime. The prospective vandal could also, at least notionally, be bought off by a sufficiently large sum offered in lieu.

Despite the fact that it may be difficult in many instances to deduce directly the value that offenders derive from certain sorts of offence, there may be indirect measures that can be used. If it is assumed that offenders do indeed compare costs and benefits, then it should be possible to infer something about the value of benefits from the reaction of individuals to changes in costs. According to our economic theory, a reduction in the costs associated with a particular crime may be expected to raise the number of such crimes committed. The *extent* of the increase in the volume of crime that results from a given change in costs may be used to make, at least a few, inferences about the benefits derived by criminals from such offences. If there is a large change in the incidence of the crime, this would suggest that for many people, the benefit from committing the offence lies somewhere between the size of the costs faced by offenders before and after the change in costs.

Costs to the Criminal

Having said something about the value of the benefits that prospective offenders may expect from committing crime, we turn next to the costs that they may expect to incur. The costs associated with criminal activity, at least as far as the criminal himself is concerned, may be broken down into two components. The first part is the probability which the offender assigns to being successfully convicted, and the second is the size of the penalty that will be imposed in the event of conviction.

The probability of conviction itself comes in two parts, the first being the probability of being caught and the second being the (conditional) probability that having once been caught, prosecution will lead to conviction. It is important to distinguish between these two contingencies, for when it comes to discussion about the policy implications of our approach, it will become clear that these probabilities stand to be influenced by quite different agencies, namely enforcers and sentencers. In each case, the probability that is relevant is the *subjective* probability, that is the view taken by the prospective criminal himself. These probability measures may diverge from the objective probabilities that an omniscient observer would rely upon. This may be important to the extent that it may suggest that efforts be directed towards influencing the subjective probabilities that individuals hold as well as to the objective probabilities determined by law enforcement and other agencies.

The second main component of the prospective cost to the criminal of his offence is the size of punishment that he receives. To the extent that there are many different forms of punishment to which the convicted offender may be sentenced, it may appear that there are insuperable problems of comparability. Whilst the size of a fine that is payable immediately may be unambiguous, in what terms is the prospective offender to measure a custodial term or a fine that is payable in instalments? This question however is much more difficult for an outsider to answer than it is for the would-be offender.

Most people could probably answer hypothetical questions of the kind: given a choice between a £50,000 fine and 5 years in prison, which would you take? It does not seem unreasonable to suggest that prospective offenders, who presumably think more about such questions than others, will be able to produce answers. Provided that the individuals can make a whole series of answers to similar questions, it follows that they can assign a figure to any sentence that may be passed. It may emerge for example that an offender would prefer 6 months' probation to a £50 fine but would prefer to pay the fine if the term of probation were extended. In such an instance, one could argue that the cost of six months' probation to such an offender could be inferred at around £50.

Obviously, the critical points at which offenders will switch allegiances between different types of sentence will vary with the offender: rich offenders will generally be more inclined to opt for fines whilst offenders who are scratching around to make a living will not need much encouragement to opt for prison. This is not to say however that rich offenders will *necessarily* opt for a fine in preference to prison or that poor offenders will do the reverse.

The other difficulty that may confront the offender is uncertainty about the type of sentence that he will receive or its size. Thus whilst he may have a clear idea of how he values different non-fine sentences, the prospective offender may find it difficult to calculate the sentence that a court will, in the event, impose upon him. Again however this difficulty is probably more apparent than real. If prospective offenders read local newspapers or listen to local radio, and in particular if they gossip with others who have been convicted in the past, they will probably find it relatively easy to establish the course of action that a court would take against them in the event of conviction.

The prospective offender is by this time well-enough informed to make a fairly accurate assessment. He has simply to compare the benefits that he expects to derive with the costs: if the former exceed the latter we may expect him to proceed, whilst in any other event he will refrain. Two questions remain, the first being how to combine the two components of the cost calculation and the second being a technical problem that flows from a comparison between a safe plan (stay at home) and a plan with uncertain consequences (commit the crime).

In order to combine the two probabilities and the size of the punishment to obtain an overall cost figure, it is necessary simply to multiply the probabilities by each other and the resulting figure by the financial equivalent of the punishment. To give an example, let us suppose that a man is thinking of stealing a car that he can resell to an accomplice for £500. Let us further suppose that he estimates the probability of getting caught to be 40 per cent, the probability of being convicted having been caught as 90 per cent and the cost to him of the six-month prison sentence that he will receive if convicted as being £1,000. The expected cost he calculates to be {0.4 x 0.9 x 1,000}, namely £360, and thus he decides to go ahead and steal the car because the benefits of £500 exceed the cost.

The technical problem that arises is the question of the prospective offender's attitude towards risk. As was shown in the discussion of uncertainty in chapter 3, individuals are likely to vary in the terms upon which they will assume risks. In the present example, a risk-neutral individual would directly compare the benefits of £500 with the expected costs of £360, and even if expected costs were to rise to £499 he would still go ahead. It is often suggested however that many people are risk averse, that is to say that they will pay a positive premium in order to be able to pursue a safe course of action rather than an uncertain one. Such individuals would thus require that the benefits would have to outweigh the costs by some positive margin if they were to be persuaded to commit the crime: they may avoid committing the crime unless the costs are less than £350 or less than £400 or whatever safety margin they like to impose. It may be noted that anyone who takes out insurance premiums in everyday life can be characterised as being similarly risk averse, since they pay a premium to have a certain wealth level rather than remain open to risks, even if *on average* this latter course would offer the lowest expected cost. Although it is sometimes suggested that criminals will often be risk preferrers – that is that they will positively enjoy the prospect of danger and uncertainty – it may simply be that those who actually commit crimes are less risk averse than others. It may alternatively be that the minority of people who choose to commit crime do so, not because they have different attitudes to risk from the remainder of the population, but because they take a more optimistic view of the probabilities of capture and conviction, or because they assign lower costs to punishment or even because they are 'better' at deriving benefits from crime.

It is difficult to establish whether this economic model of the decisions people make about whether or not to commit crime is more or less good at predicting crime rates, and perhaps more importantly, predicting how crime rates would respond to changes in enforcement or sentencing policy, than are the more traditional models of criminal behaviour that emphasize social factors of various kinds. Considerable efforts have been expended by criminologists and also by economists in trying to establish whether the variables stressed in the economic model, in which deterrence plays the dominant role, are more or less reliable guides to crime rates than are other factors. In some recent work on crime in the UK, Carr-Hill and Stern (1979), using some very elaborate statistical techniques, seem to conclude that the deterrence model stands up relatively well. Measuring the likelihood of conviction by the clear-up or conviction rate, and the severity of punishment by reference to the proportion of offenders being imprisoned (greater severity being indicated by a higher proportion being imprisoned), Carr-Hill and Stern established that these two variables were for the most part important factors in determining the rate of offending (Carr-Hill and Stern, op cit, pp. 231-236). They suggest that these results conform with the consensus view, and in support of this quote from Votey (1969) who argues that: 'The decline in police effectiveness, as measured by the ratio of offences cleared by arrest to known offences (clearance ratio) . . has encouraged criminality and induced higher rates of growth in *per capita* offence rates' (p 3). They claim further support from the work of Swimmer (1974) and Silver (1974).

What, in any event, *is* clear is that if the probabilities of conviction and the size of punishment *do* influence crime rates, then decision makers have something to go on: there do exist control variables that can be adjusted in such a way as to influence the volume of crime that takes place. If this is the case, then the next question is how society is to choose the volume of crime that it wishes to take place, and in order for this question to be tackled, it is essential first to take note that there may be costs generated by crime and its prevention that do not enter the calculus of the individual offender, but that will nevertheless influence society's decision.

DECISIONS ABOUT THE CONTROL OF CRIME

The major object of this next section is twofold: first to illustrate that the cost-benefit calculations relevant to society in this area will differ markedly from the cost-benefit calculations relevant to offenders, and secondly to illustrate that since the control of crime is likely to itself be a costly activity it is unlikely that society will want to devote resources to crime prevention up to the point where crime is completely eliminated.

Damage Costs

There are two main classes of costs that crime imposes upon society. The first is the category of costs that result directly from the damage inflicted by crime. This will include the value of property that is damaged or destroyed and the value of human injury and death that is caused by crime. It will *exclude* the value of goods that are stolen, since such crimes do not affect the volume of resources available to society in total, only the distribution of these resources amongst society. Theft need not however always be costless: if the thief damages the goods as he steals them, or if theft becomes so prevalent as to reduce the incentives to accumulate physical assets, such losses may be regarded as costs, for they do reduce the society's stock of assets either now or later.

Theft is not the only example of an instance where the cost of a crime is *not* measured by the extent of the immediate loss to the victim. There are some activities that appear to involve something like a cost, but would not be thought, by some economists at least, to constitute a criminal activity because

the 'losses' are confined to the individual involved in the
activity. If I enjoy smashing crockery in my own home and
do not affect anyone as a result, there are no cost
implications for the rest of society. That I will as a result
'consume' more crockery than my neighbours is no more a
matter for society's concern than would be the fact that I eat
more bread than others or buy fewer cabbages. If on the
other hand I go around throwing cups and saucers through
shop windows, or at passers-by, others are involved and my
activities become a matter of concern. The definition of the
costs flowing from criminal activity therefore includes
everything except those costs borne by the criminal himself.
This is of course a rather liberal conception of the notion of
cost and it may have some consequences that more
paternalistic decision-makers find abhorrent. It seems to
imply that frequently-outlawed sexual activities that take
place between mutually consenting parties in private may be
essentially costless, as might the private consumption of
certain sorts of prohibited drugs. The only possible counter
to this argument is that such activities may at least *potentially*
be costly for the rest of society in the sense that participants
in such activities are liable to subsequently corrupt and
pervert others. Without pursuing this rather delicate
argument further, it is clear that some 'costs' may be easier to
identify than others.

Difficulties of measuring costs are likely to arise in the
context of offences against the person. Personal injuries or
simply the fear of personal injury may make life extremely
unpleasant for people. If people believe that 'the streets are
unsafe at night', then there will presumably be frequent
occasions on which they forego activities that they would
pursue if they felt more secure.

It is possible however to let some of these difficulties seem
to become more severe than they really are. There are many
instances in which society confronts difficult decisions in
which human life and limb may be at issue. The building of
new roads or hospitals for example are likely to have
consequences for the number of injuries caused and the
number of lives saved. When such decisions are made, values

are either implicitly or explicitly put on human suffering. Whilst this may seem unpalatable it is unavoidable in a world in which there are insufficient resources to do everything that we would like: for comment see Glover (1977), Mooney (1977) or Calabresi & Babbitt (1978). The problem arises also in the context of personal injury and death in a civil law context. Under the tort system, judges are constantly making compensation awards to victims, so again values are being put on losses that might at first blush seem to be incalculable. Equally, the notion of giving (financial) compensation to victims of crime seems to be increasing in popularity, yielding another source of information about the sorts of values that may be assigned to particular sorts of injury.

Control Costs

The second main class of costs entailed by the occurrence of crime is generated by prevention and enforcement activities that give rise to control costs. Resources that are used to combat crime could be used for more genuinely productive activities if the prospect of crime were absent. Calculations about the social cost of crime will have to take account of such costs, since they represent opportunities foregone. It is important also to distinguish between those costs of crime prevention and enforcement which are incurred by the individual prospective victim and those which are incurred collectively via the tax/public expenditure system.

Looking first at the volume of private cost it is possible to identify some crime prevention services which are bought through the market, and others which involve the individual taking direct precautions of various kinds. When firms move pay-rolls around, or are delivering precious consignments of goods, they are quite likely to employ the services of a company that specialises in such provision. The specialised equipment, vehicles and personnel that private security firms have are designed to make theft or whatever more difficult and the probability of capture of thieves higher, in order that the likelihood of the theft of any particular consignment may be reduced. Security firms may of course also be retained to provide personal protection or to install burglar alarms. It is perhaps interesting to note in passing that burglar alarms may either be displayed prominently on houses or vehicles in an attempt to deter the prospective criminal who might be 'casing the joint', or that they may be less obtrusive and designed to alert the police that a burglary is taking place, so that there is an improved chance of making a red-handed arrest. Expenditure on security provisions of the kind so far outlined is in principle relatively easy to measure, since market transactions are taking place. Much less easy to measure is the cost implied by the preventive activities upon which individuals or firms themselves engage. Householders and car owners generally lock their property when they leave it. This may often be inconvenient and time-consuming and thus again it represents a cost since it is a course of action that would not be followed save for the prospect of a crime being committed.

The publicly-borne components of crime costs may be relatively straightforward to identify, at an aggregate level at least. Police activities in the detection and prosecution of criminals are an obvious example. Less obvious is the role of police patrols, if any, in reducing the *total* amount of crimes committed. This role will be minimal if it simply affects the particular crimes committed and drives criminals into the less intensively-policed areas. It will be significant if it is successful in persuading prospective criminals that the probability of their being caught if they commit crime is higher than they would otherwise suppose. Many police officers do not however spend all or most of their time on crime-related work. Traffic control is an example of police work that falls into the non-crime category, and it may very often be difficult if not impossible to apportion police costs amongst traffic, crime detection and prevention and other activities. A single officer on patrol may confront a wide variety of possible demands on his time on a particular day, and any attempt to pin down his allocation of time amongst the different types of work will be fraught with difficulty. Despite this, it is possible that a determined researcher could establish a rough idea of the proportion of police time and resources devoted to non-criminal work and apply the appropriate adjustment to the figures for national expenditure on police services.

An Example

Having restricted ourselves so far to discussion at a purely general level, it might be illuminating at this point to consider a particular example. Amongst the attractions of using such an example is that in addition to requiring a list of costs to be drawn up, it very naturally suggests the further question of who actually bears the costs. Although we have so far ignored this aspect of the costs question, it should quickly become clear that it may be a major concern.

Imagine a shopkeeper who owns a single shop and employs two or three assistants to help him run it. The shopkeeper is conscious that he may be the target of several different sorts of crime: shoplifting by customers, dishonesty of his staff and theft of his stock and/or takings are his three main worries; what precautions should he take? In the case of shoplifting, there are various possibilities, but chiefly the installation of mirrors and other devices (possibly closed-circuit TV) and the use of store detectives. Each of these possibilities will be quite expensive, but if he knows that shoplifting will otherwise be a major problem he may find one or more of these policies to be expedient. If he is a profit-maximizer, the shopkeeper will in each case decide whether to use the prevention device or not by comparing the reduction in losses from shoplifting with the cost of the device.

In the case of possible dishonesty amongst staff, the problem is more subtle. Since it is likely that the shopkeeper will find it difficult to catch staff in the act of dishonesty, he may react by operating a very careful policy about who he takes on as assistants. By asking for references, enquiring into a person's local reputation, personal interview and reference to various personal characteristics, the shopkeeper may aim to filter out the less reliable. He may then decide that the person who is asking for a higher wage rate to do the job may be a better bet than someone who is prepared to do it at the wage offered. An alternative policy is to take assistants on initially at a relatively low wage but to offer them the prospect of regular increases provided that no dishonesty occurs. A less widely used policy would be to offer employees a profit-related bonus. The difficulty with this is likely to be that such a bonus would probably be an insufficient incentive to dissuade a determined assistant from theft.

As far as break-ins to the shop are concerned, the shopkeeper will probably act in much the same way as a private householder. Depending on the requirements imposed by his insurance policy, we may presume that he will try quite hard to avoid being burgled, by fitting secure locks and catches and so on. Note however that there may still be precautions that could be taken that ordinary shopkeepers generally do not take. Nightwatchmen, barred windows, very heavy safes and individual security covers for different sets of merchandise are all precautions that are available, but for the average shopkeeper do not offer a rate of return over their cost that is sufficient to make them attractive.

If for simplicity we ignore any other sorts of crime to which the shopkeeper may be subject, we can draw a number of conclusions from the findings so far. In the first place, each of the three types of crime is likely to give rise to some preventive activity by the shopkeeper. In each case he will compare the costs and benefits of different policies and choose those that are most conducive to his profits. The costs that he does incur will be borne in part by him in the form of lower profits than he would earn if such crimes did not threaten and partly in the form of higher prices to consumers than he would otherwise charge. The balance between those costs absorbed by the shopkeeper and those absorbed by the consumer will depend upon the degree to which retailing is a competitive industry and upon the characteristics of consumer demand. There is however an important caveat. The role of public crime prevention or law enforcement agencies has been ignored up to this point in our shopkeeper example. We have made the implicit assumption that the public sector activity level is given and that the shopkeeper is doing his calculations accordingly. If there were to be a change in public sector policing levels, then the shopkeeper would have to redo his calculations.

Suppose for example that police patrols in the area of the shop were doubled. This would raise the probability of apprehension for those considering breaking into the shop, and by thus reducing the likelihood of a break-in might well induce the shopkeeper to reduce his security precautions. He may now for example only bank his takings once a week instead of three times or whatever. But of course the net effect on crime may move in either direction, since the prospective haul for thieves is now higher even if the chance of getting caught has risen. The change in public sector activity thus affects private sector activity: in the example the rise in public sector policing will mean increased public expenditure, whilst the resulting reduction in private anti-crime measures will reduce private expenditure, and will be reflected in either lower prices for consumers and/or higher profits for the shopkeeper. The important implication therefore is that public and private anti-crime activities may *de facto* operate as substitutes, reductions in one generating increases in the other and vice versa.

OPTIMAL POLICY

The analysis so far has been positive rather than normative: we have been seeking to answer questions of the form: what would happen if the penalties associated with crime were to change, or what would happen if public expenditure on the police were changed? By collecting enough facts and figures it should be possible to get some way towards answering these questions. The final stage for discussion here is more controversial, and strays into areas in which value judgments are made, implicitly or explicitly, about the distribution of wealth amongst society, or, what amounts to the same thing, about the relative deservedness of different individuals in the population. The decision that remains to be made comes really in two parts: first, what is the appropriate level for expenditure upon anti-crime measures in total and secondly, what is the appropriate balance to strike between expenditure by public and private agencies?

In both cases, it is possible here only to give some idea of the general principles upon which such decisions might be based. The question of the overall level of spending, it may be argued, should be determined by a comparison of the overall costs and benefits associated with different levels of crime. In foregoing sections, it has been shown that as the level of anti-crime measures changes (that is, the level of expenditure by both public and private agencies taken together), so too does the volume of crime committed; if this were not true, there would presumably be no police force and no private preventive activities. At the same time, changes in the level of crime committed will change the volume of damage costs flowing from crime: more crimes means more losses from damage.

The cost-benefit calculation entails comparing the two different sorts of costs. This is readily illustrated as in figure 4.1 in which both categories of cost are related to the level of crime being committed. The schedule TC is derived by adding vertically, at each level of crime, the two different sorts of

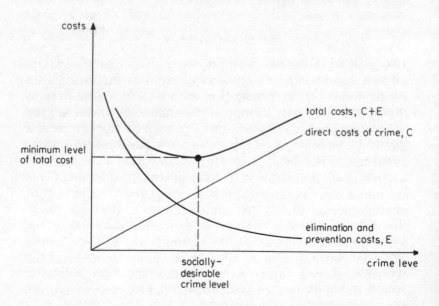

Figure 4.1 Costs and the 'Optimal' Level of Crime

cost. The assumptions made in the diagram are that prevention plus enforcement (or 'control') costs rise very rapidly as we seek to eliminate crime altogether (the conventional assumption of increasing marginal cost), and that extra units of crime generate costs at a steady rate. The consequence of making these two assumptions is that the total cost schedule has a U-shape. It is then but a short step to move to the conclusion that the desired level of crime will be the one that minimises overall costs, that is the level at which the trough of the U-shaped TC schedule occurs. To describe this level of crime as the 'socially desirable' level of crime may require us to make judgments about income distribution, and may seem counter-intuitive. Any other level of crime will however involve yet higher costs, and in particular it can be seen that the increasingly heavy expenditure on control that must occur as we get to low levels of crime will not be offset by countervailing reductions in the losses that crime is creating.

The second part of the decision that has to be made concerns the balance between public and private spending on prevention and enforcement. The schedule which relates these costs to the volume of crime contains a sleight of hand that conceals the fact that the answer to this question must already be known. It has been assumed in drawing the diagram that the control costs associated with a given level of crime embody an 'efficient' mix of public and private activities. In other words the cost is given as the lowest possible total of private plus public spending that is consistent with that particular level of crime.

CONCLUSION AND SUMMARY

The view of criminal behaviour and of the desirable level of criminal activity that has been advanced here differs in many respects from the conventional wisdom. The major disadvantages of this economics-based approach are to be found in the relatively simplistic treatment of the decision about whether to commit crime or not and in the rather heavy demands that such an approach puts upon inputs of empirical information. The compensating advantages that result derive from the fact that one has a basic picture of crime and the criminal that may be applied systematically to virtually any policy question. It becomes possible to think of sentencing policy and enforcement policy as being complementary rather than distinct concerns: it becomes clear that the impact of changes in the behaviour of the public sector of crime control will depend upon the interactions between the public and private sectors, and so on. The following chapters take up some more familiar issues that arise in the administration of the public sector of crime prevention and enforcement, and rely at a number of points upon arguments that have been developed in the present chapter.

We began this chapter by looking at how an individual may come to a decision about whether or not to commit crime. It was suggested that such a decision could be approached in the same kind of way as the more conventional sorts of choices that individuals are continually making as consumers or workers. Prospective criminals may be characterised as weighing up the costs and benefits of crime and comparing these returns with those available under alternative courses of action. The second half of the chapter was concerned with the decision confronting society about how many resources it is to devote to the control of crime. It was suggested that this issue could be resolved by comparing the costs associated with crime control on the one hand and those associated with the damage or harm imposed by crime on the other. It was suggested that this trade-off could in principle be resolved, although it might be exceedingly difficult to gather together the plethora of information that would ideally be required.

FURTHER READING

The suggestion that decisions to commit crime can be thought of in just the same way as decisions about legitimate activities is not new. The modern variant of the suggestion, in which attitude to risk and responses to changes in the level of policing (inter alia) are stressed, is due largely to Becker (1968). The idea was further pursued by Ehrlich (1973). More recent discussions are to be found in Anderson (1976) and Carr-Hill and Stern (1979). The works mentioned thus far have in common a heavily formal approach which makes them very difficult for non-specialists, despite the relatively straightforward ideas upon which they are based. For a more accessible treatment, see Culyer (1973) or Baldry (1974).

5

The Economics of Punishment

The previous chapter sets out the different sorts of costs that crime might generate and the cost-benefit calculus that prospective criminals confront. The object of this chapter is to use these findings as a starting point for an investigation of some of the issues that confront policy-makers in the area of 'law and order'.

It may be useful at the outset to point out that a wide range of public bodies will be involved, and that a wide range of different types of decision will be involved. Executive agencies like the police force will be concerned, since the decisions made within the police about the disposal of available resources will influence which sorts of laws are most rigorously enforced. Legislative agencies will play a part, since Parliament decides upon matters like the definition of different sorts of crimes. In addition, the judiciary, as the third branch of government will obviously be involved, both in the interpretation of law as well as in the passing of judgment and sentence upon offenders.

It should also be emphasized that the decisions taken by all three types of government body will have a great variety of implications for those who are considering committing crime. The disposal of police resources will affect the probability of being caught; the statutes will govern whether an activity is to be labelled 'criminal' and the size of the maximum penalty that may be applied, whilst the sentencing policy adopted by the judiciary will influence both the probability that a person standing trial will be convicted, and the type and severity of the penalties imposed upon conviction.

In this chapter our main concern is to isolate a handful of main issues at different stages in what might be termed the 'punishment process', and to show how economic thinking might be brought to bear. It is readily conceded that the application of economics does not provide instant answers to any of the difficult sorts of decisions that are discussed in this chapter: some at least of the issues have been widely debated by commentators for a very long time, and it would be fatuous to imagine that simple solutions lie just around the corner.

ALLOCATING POLICE RESOURCES

It is difficult to imagine a world in which police resources are sufficient to detect and solve all the crimes committed. In some instances this may be because of insuperable problems: the trail has gone cold and there are no clues to be had. More often however it will simply not be judged expedient to try and solve all crimes, even if there is no real reason why a sufficiently intensive effort should not throw up sufficient clues and evidence in any single case considered in isolation. It comes as a nasty shock to some people who are burgled to find that the police do not immediately mount a major search to track down the villain who has run off with their television set. At the other end of the spectrum however, large-scale robberies and notorious murders may attract an extremely intensive police effort. These rather casual observations suggest that when it comes to the allocation of resources for attempts to 'solve' crime, greater efforts will be made in those instances where the crime is seen as more serious, because it involves theft of larger amounts, because it involves murder or whatever. An appropriate balance of effort may be achieved in practice by the use of rules of thumb: thefts of sums less than some particular amount may be simply recorded and no active steps taken: thefts of larger amounts, or instances where it is thought that a series of thefts by the same individual or gang is involved, may be assigned to a detective whilst more serious crime attracts attention at a higher level and involves several men locally and possibly also a team of specialists who are sent in from a regional or national centre.

It may be tempting to think that reliance upon relatively crude decision rules about how much effort to devote to an enquiry represents a rather ad hoc approach to catching criminals, and that such decisions do not really resemble closely the solutions to elaborate equations of the kind that economists are prone to write down. Such a view may well be mistaken however.

In the first place, it may well be inefficient in an economic sense to have very sophisticated decision rules about what actions to take in day-to-day events. The Chief Constable or local police chief rightly, will not want to be bothered entering discussion about whether a particular offence should be taken more or less seriously. The existence of customary practice in conjunction with more or less explicit rules of thumb and the good sense of experienced officers can for the most part be relied upon to allocate the limited resources available to the police reasonably sensibly. That is to say that although an omniscient Chief Constable may observe that mistakes are being made, he may nevertheless be satisfied that the measures needed to reduce the volume of mistakes would involve much more cumbersome administrative procedures that absorbed more manpower than could be justified by the improved allocation of manpower amongst the available tasks.

The other important reason why relatively straightforward decision rules may be valuable is more subtle. Recall from the previous chapter that decisions to become an offender depend upon the probability of being caught, other things being equal. Now it is likely that the crimes that society is most anxious to *prevent* are those that involve the greatest costs, be it in terms of physical injury or property damage. If a prospective criminal knows that he will be more vigorously pursued if he commits an offence that imposes high costs than if he commits some more trivial offence, he may be induced to opt for the latter rather than the former. The importance of there being a systematic relation between the seriousness of a crime and the extent of the police reaction lies therefore in the likelihood that offenders will be persuaded that they run a greater likelihood of arrest (again, other things being equal) the more damaging is their offence.

In arguing as we do here that the pattern of enforcement is critical because of its potential *deterrence* value rather than because it reflects a more *just* response to the crime that has been committed, we are relying to a great extent on the principle that 'bygones are bygones'. Once a crime has been committed, the damage has been done, the costs have been incurred and there is no way that the damage can be undone. Even if the criminal is caught and required to compensate the victim, the net loss has already been incurred. It cannot therefore be argued that there is any prospect of reducing costs by tracking down the criminal. The only way of reducing the costs that crimes of this kind impose is to find ways of preventing such crimes being committed in the first place. Although the offender and the victim in any particular case will be concerned about whether the offender is caught, the major concern of the rest of society is likely to be that 'too much' crime of this kind is being committed or that 'too few' arrests are being made of those committing such offences. Such judgments may in some respects be ill-informed, but they are consistent with the view that it is the prospective deterrent value of capturing criminals rather than the value of punishing the guilty that motivates enforcement activities.

The important implication of the deterrence argument is that the pattern of enforcement activities will be designed to minimise the overall costs of crime and not necessarily to maximise the likelihood that people committing some particular form of crime are caught. To this extent it will be important to have at least a rough idea of the sensitivity of prospective criminals to intensification of police efforts. It may for example be suggested that there are certain sorts of offence in which even quite large changes in the vigour of enforcement will be largely irrelevant. In many instances of murder within families it may be conjectured that 'psychological' factors will be a much more important determinant of the number of deaths that occur than will be the expenditure of police energies on enquiries in such cases. If this suspicion were shown to have some foundation, then it might be argued that heavy expenditure on solving such crimes might not produce much of a return in terms of a reduction in the number of such offences committed subsequently. An occasional unsolved murder case of this kind may be more than offset by the reduction in the incidence of rape or some other category of offence on which police efforts may now be concentrated.

It must be conceded at this point that the economic view of the allocation of police resources is in some important ways rather idealised. Whilst decisions made within police forces about how resources are allocated to solving particular sorts of crime (and about how resources are allocated between crime-solving and other sorts of police work), *may* conform to the deterrence model that we have outlined in general, it may differ from it in certain instances. This is really like saying that although it is generally convenient to assume that firms set out to maximise profits, there may be some circumstances in which they actually pursue some different objective. There are two relatively straightforward cases in which police allocation decisions may differ from those that an omniscient social planner wishing to minimise the social costs of crime and punishment would make.

The first possible cause of discrepancy is likely to be that police performance, in so far as it is judged, may be measured by criteria that are not consistent with the minimising of social cost. It seems likely for example that if the quality of policing is to be assessed, it will be done by reference to factors such as the proportion of crimes that have been cleared up, or in the number of arrests per officer or something along similar lines. The reason why such measures are used is of course that relatively objective, historical accounts may be obtained of the number of crimes recorded, the number of instances where arrests or court appearances were made, the value of stolen property recovered and so on. For reasons discussed earlier however statistics of this kind may be inconclusive or positively misleading, since they make no mention of deterrence effects. Such figures do not really measure therefore whether police activities have been well-directed or not. Nevertheless, it is important that the police are put in a position where they are forced to account for themselves, since if they were allowed to do whatever they liked on the grounds that they were the only ones who were really in a position to make sound judgments about the social cost minimising pattern of activities, much greater dangers might arise. Police views of social cost may differ from society's views, and there may be pressures for allocative decisions to be oriented in ways that were to the advantage of police officers and the disadvantage of the rest of society. The privileged position of the police in some dictatorships seems on occasion to lead to excesses of various kinds that could hardly be thought of as being in the best interests of society as a whole. Thus the public accountability of the police may be accorded a very high priority in democratic societies even if this may sometimes entail the use of indicators of performance that are not consistent with the pursuit of a pattern of enforcement that minimises overall costs.

The second possible cause of discrepancy between the objectives of the police and the 'economic' objective results from the likelihood that the police, along with society at large, may sometimes pursue *retribution* as well as deterrence. Society and the police may feel unusually outraged by some particular offence and may go to great lengths to find the guilty party: to lengths that may not be justified by the likely deterrent effect on future crime of their activity. When this occurs, resources will be misdirected according to the economic model. There are however economists (Adelstein, 1980, being one) who would argue that retribution does have an important role to play, and that models which exclude it are unlikely to be very good at explaining what is happening in the real world. Accountability is probably particularly important in such instances, since there is much greater scope for police to misinterpret the wishes of their sponsors.

Despite the caveats that have just been discussed, it remains clear that the analysis of the previous chapter which identified different sorts of costs associated with crime can be exploited to produce a model upon which enforcement activities may be based. It is perhaps asking too much to expect that law enforcement agencies will always be governed by such principles, but on the other hand, such a model does produce a set of idealised criteria that can be used as a starting point in the discussion of enforcement.

It has been argued, at least implicitly, in this section that the allocation of police resources will be based to a greater or lesser degree on the criterion of minimising total social cost. In practical terms decisions about the allocation of police resources will be reflected in the amount of their time that police officers assign to different sorts of activity, in the way in which police cars are used, in the relative amounts of expenditure on capital terms such as radios, cars, surveillance equipment, anti-riot equipment and so on. Another facet of resource use within the police service will be the size of the force employed in different areas. The size of the 'establishment', that is the desired number of officers in different regions may reflect local variations in the pattern or volume of crime, in the extent to which the region is urbanised, in the size of the population and so forth. Whilst it seems unlikely that the administrative decisions taken on resource allocation will explicitly rely upon economic arguments of the kind put forward here, they may well bear a close resemblance to the decisions that such arguments would suggest. If this is *not* true, then one is forced to start from scratch in the search for some alternative model of policy, and probably one that relies on rather ad hoc notions such as administrative expedience or historical accident.

The allocative decisions made by police forces will influence crime. Although the police may attempt to conceal some elements of their anti-crime strategies in an attempt to keep the criminal guessing, it is inevitable that criminals will learn how police work and come to anticipate their activities. The pattern of crime actually observed will thus be influenced by the interaction between criminal and law enforcer. Changes in the allocation of police resources will cause criminals to review their activities whilst a change in criminal behaviour is likely to trigger off an adjustment in the way in which police resources are used. A similar kind of tension is likely to exist between police decision-makers, those engaged in sentencing and the criminal. Changes in sentencing policy may for example influence both criminals and police, and it is to these sorts of interactions that we now turn.

SENTENCING POLICY

For the criminal who has been arrested or is considering the consequences of arrest, the major concern will probably be the sentence that he will receive. Ignoring any stigma that being convicted of a crime may bring, or any hero-worship that convicted criminals may attract, the severity of the punishment handed down by the court will be the central concern. The main decisions that those sitting in judgment have to make concern first whether or not to convict on the evidence presented, and in the event of conviction both the type and size of the penalty to be imposed.

It is probably fair to say that sentencing policy generally gives rise to more controversy than any other single issue in the criminal justice system. For various reasons, many participants in the debate have strongly-held views about the way that convicted offenders should be treated, views that often differ very widely. At one end of the spectrum is the view that those who commit crime are deliberately and flagrantly rejecting the rules of society and should be treated as outcasts. This 'hang 'em and flog 'em' approach tends to be associated with high levels of expenditure on prisons. At the other end of the spectrum is the view that so-called crime can generally be traced back to an individual's exploitation at the hands of a wicked society: the appropriate response is to reorganise or revolutionise society in such a way as to eradicate the causes of criminal activity.

The major lesson that economics can offer to the discussion of sentencing policy is the distinction between the deterrence value and other costs and benefits of different policies. In the economic model the object of punishment is *deterrence* and not (usually at any rate) *retribution*. The sentence is not viewed as representing society's displeasure at what has happened in the case at issue, since the damage already done cannot be undone, but rather represents a warning to those considering committing such offences in the future. The choice between alternative sentences thus depends primarily on which may be expected to have the greatest deterrent effect on would-be criminals. This choice does however have to take into account the *enforcement* costs associated with different penalties. That is to say that it may be possible to think of sentences that have very attractive deterrence properties but that are prohibitively (or just relatively) expensive to administer.

It is worth mentioning that most criminologists distinguish between two different types of deterrent effect that may result, either intentionally or accidentally, from sentencing decisions. *Specific* deterrence refers to the effects that a sentence may have upon the person committing an offence: will the punishment discourage that particular individual from committing crime in the future? *General* deterrence on the other hand refers to the impact that the sentence may have upon other prospective offenders. This distinction may well be important in certain instances but is not one that has very deep implications in the rather general discussion here.

It would perhaps be well to mention also that economic models in this area tend to ignore the possibility that certain forms of sentence have a *rehabilitative* role and that a period of imprisonment may in some circumstances influence the way that an offender will behave after leaving prison. It is however difficult to establish convincingly that punishment may somehow induce offenders to 'learn from their mistakes'. Such effects could really only be expected if it were thought that criminals systematically underestimate the unpleasantness of the sentences that they potentially bring upon themselves when committing crime, and that the only way a particular offender will learn to take the threat of punishment seriously is to give him first-hand experience of it.

Economic models tend to neglect also the *incapacitative* effect of custody. In the case of those offenders who are adjudged to represent a 'threat to society', a potential cost to society may be removed if the individual in question is locked away. Such arguments contain many potential pitfalls and in particular may encourage the view that there are some people who ought to be locked up even if they have not as yet actually been convicted of an offence. It is in any event likely to be difficult as in the case of ·the debate about rehabilitation, to establish reliable prognoses of how an individual will behave both now and in the future if imprisoned and how this compares with his behaviour if he is not imprisoned.

Leaving aside rehabilitation, retribution and incapacitation, we concentrate in what follows on the trade-off between deterrent value and enforcement costs. For simplicity, we further concentrate on the choice between fines and imprisonment as alternative sentences and investigate some of the associated costs. As a first step we investigate the costs of imprisonment, and then move to the choice between fines and prison.

Looking first at prison, costs may be seen to include the costs of building and running prisons. Whilst these costs may be substantial in themselves, it must be remembered that costs may also be generated if those in prison would otherwise be working and thus contributing to national output. If offenders would otherwise be unemployed and idle such costs may be small, but particularly at times when unemployment is not widespread and particularly in the case of offenders who are unusually valuable workers, such costs may be very high. In any event, prisons are expensive to run since they tend to be extremely labour-intensive. With the contraction through time in the length of the working week and the advent of technical innovation, most industries come to use many fewer hours of labour per unit of output. In the case of prisons however the shorter working week means that more prison officers are needed to look after a given block of cells, thereby reducing the ratio of inmates to staff. The possibilities for introducing labour-saving technology have been rare, with the result that the prison service has been taking on additional labour. To give some idea of the rate at which the prison sector has been absorbing resources, a study published recently (Shaw, 1980) showed that whilst public expenditure as a whole had increased elevenfold over the period 1956 to 1978, expenditure on prisons over the same period increased 29 fold. The same study noted at different points that 'non-custodial sanctions are in most cases much cheaper than sentences of imprisonment' and that there had been 'a lack of interest hitherto paid to economic criteria by those responsible for penal policy'.

Increases in the costs of imprisonment need however to be put in perspective. If sentencers are to be discouraged from committing offenders to prison it is necessary to know what alternatives are available and how costly they are. Fines, on the surface at least, are an extremely attractive, cheap alternative to imprisonment. Imposing a fine does not prevent an individual from working as does prison − indeed it may provide a positive incentive to the offender in that by working longer hours than he did before conviction he may be able to pay off the fine without incurring a major fall in his living standard. In addition, fines do not involve heavy expenditures on public buildings and staff: the major requirement is simply a recording office, and a reminders procedure for those who have been ordered to pay. The problem however is that some of those who are fined may persistently fail to pay up, and clearly some kind of back-up arrangements are required in such instances. This ultimately means imprisonment if successive reminders and enquiries fail to induce payment. Indeed the importance of this observation is underlined by the fact that the most rapidly growing section of the prison population has been that of fine defaulters (Home Office, 1979). Morgan and Bowles (1981) observe that the number of people imprisoned for fine default is running at approximately 17,000 per annum and that this is more than twice the number which prevailed in 1967 when the Criminal Justice Act was passed with the object of reducing resort to custody in the enforcement of fines.

The reasons for this rapid increase in the incidence of default can be traced partly to the fact that the fine is being more widely used than it was previously. This has meant, inter alia, that offenders who would have been imprisoned some years ago are now being fined. These 'marginal' offenders may as a group be less reliable than those who have traditionally been fined. What is of more concern however is the likelihood that if sentencers were to extend yet further their reliance on fines, the incidence of default may rise yet again. In instances where there is a high likelihood that an offender will fail to pay a fine then the sentencer is faced with the options of accepting that the offender may well end up in jail if fined or of reducing the size of the fine that he is to impose. In the case of offenders who are unemployed or poorly-paid, this may mean imposing fines that sound absurdly low or in some cases of imposing prison sentences for apparently trivial offences. Neither outcome is very palatable, but it is very difficult to see how sentencers can avoid such choices unless they are to have recourse to other sorts of sentence. The implication seems to be that whilst the costs of imprisonment are (and will remain) high, the costs of imposing fines have been rising rapidly and will continue to do so if sentencers extend their use of the fine still further.

The more technical details of the design of the present system of administering and enforcing fines are pursued in the following chapter. In conclusion to the present chapter, we present a summary of the activities and interactions of the various individuals and agencies who have been identified as playing a major role in the criminal justice system.

SUMMARY AND CONCLUSIONS

In the course of this chapter a succession of arguments has been used in building up a rudimentary picture of how an economist views the process of punishment. Perhaps the best way of summarising the rather tortuous path we have followed is to trace the passage of an individual from the point at which he has committed a crime through the criminal justice system. In order to stress the deterrence orientation of the economic approach, it is useful to add to this the feedback from the punishment process to the decisions being made by prospective offenders about whether or not to commit crime. Although it may seem preposterous to argue that prospective criminals can identify accurately all the information about probabilities and so forth assumed in the diagram, it is clear at the same time that individuals who commit crime are aware, if only vaguely, of the prospects of punishment. If policy-makers are contemplating changing the structure of any part of the system they need to have some way of systematically predicting the impact on crime rates and on the various categories of costs generated by crime and the criminal justice system. Figure 5.1 below incorporates the main categories of costs and illustrates how the different parts of the system interact.

To the extent that changes in any single part of the system trigger off adjustments throughout, it is difficult to draw

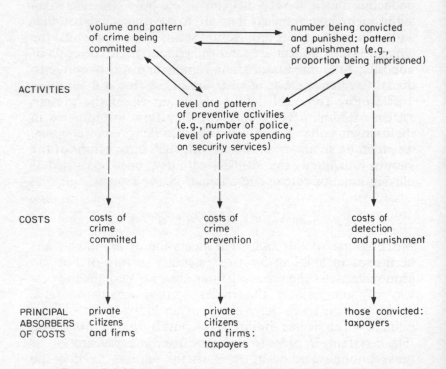

Figure 5.1 Main Elements of the Criminal Justice System

simple conclusions about the effects of different policies. Let us take as an example a stiffening of penalties for armed robbery. This is most likely to be manifest in the form of an increase in the term of imprisonment on those convicted of such offences. The immediate effect will probably be a reduction in the number of armed robberies committed. This will be accompanied by a rise in the cost of punishing those found guilty of the offence in the meantime. In the longer run, criminals may commit more unarmed robberies than before; private security arrangements may be slackened; police will spend a smaller proportion of their time on cases of armed robbery and so on. The presumption is that the system will adjust to a new equilibrium in which all parts of the system become fully tuned to the new sentencing policy. The crucial point is that whilst the final result is likely to be a reduction in the number of armed robberies, the associated adjustments may impose extra costs that exceed the reduction in the damage caused by armed robbery. To take the simplest possible case, doubling the prison term imposed may only reduce the volume of such crime committed by 40 per cent. Apart from any other considerations, this would entail an increase in expenditure upon the imprisonment of such offenders.

The main conclusion to be drawn from this chapter is that there is likely to exist a high degree of interdependence between different parts of the criminal justice system. When this is put alongside the findings of the previous chapter about the behaviour of individual criminals the natural inference is that both sentencing policy and the way in which the criminal justice system generally is administered (to which we now turn) will influence the various incentives and disincentives that prospective criminals confront and will thus influence the level and pattern of crime committed.

FURTHER READING

The deterrence approach to punishment can be traced back at least to the writings of Beccaria-Bonesana (1767). More recent discussions are to be found in Carr-Hill and Stern

(1979), especially chapter 2.2 and in Gibbs (1975). The work of Becker (1968) and Stigler (1970) forms the starting point for most contemporary economic analysis of punishment. The more particular questions of how police resources are allocated and of the objectives and costs of different sentencing policies are matters to which economists have not as yet devoted great efforts, although they have been extensively discussed by others. Of interest also is the work of Ehrlich (1972, 1975) and others who took up Ehrlich's analysis of capital punishment: see for example Baldus and Cole (1975). In recent times, particularly with increasing pressure on public spending, the economic facets of punishment have come to be taken more seriously as may be seen in two recent publications by NACRO: see NACRO (1981) and Shaw (1980).

6

The Administration of Justice

In this, the last of the chapters concerned with the criminal justice system, we take up some of the issues prompted by the administration of law and order. A variety of agencies is involved and the total costs at issue are large. Many of these agencies have considerable discretion as to how they use resources, and in a number of cases the methods of monitoring and controlling resource use raise questions about whether resources are being efficiently allocated in this sector.

It is probably best to make it clear from the start that economics does not as yet have a well-developed theory of how public sector agencies may be expected to behave. The private firm producing goods or services for sale has a clearly-identifiable 'output', and the pressures via capital markets for firms to earn as high a rate of return on resources employed as possible provide a clear framework for predicting how firms will behave and provide also a clear criterion against which decisions can be evaluated. The same is not true for public agencies like courts or prisons: they involve costs that are very difficult to quantify and further, they do not generate an output that can be readily measured. This often bedevils efforts to assess efficiency or to identify ways in which operations could be improved.

Attempts have been made to find a theory capable of explaining and predicting the behaviour of government departments but none has as yet been shown to be completely satisfactory, and none can be readily applied in the present context. The best known work on the economics of bureaucracy, Niskanen (1971), is based on the hypothesis that agency chiefs have the maximisation of their own department's operating budget as their central objective. Signs of the 'empire-building' to which such an objective can be expected to give rise may be detected in certain areas of the criminal justice system. Expenditure in England and Wales on the prison service, for example has grown very much more quickly than expenditure generally. Whilst this may be interpreted to mean that bureaucrats within the service are successful in their efforts to expand at the expense of others, it is difficult to see why this part of the public sector should have been relatively *more* successful than other parts. A persuasive model of public sector behaviour should, for example, be capable of explaining why expenditure on prisons should have grown nearly twice as quickly as expenditure on the police over the period 1956 – 78 (see Shaw, 1980).

The lack of a general model capable of explaining the behaviour of agencies is not however a disaster. Many of the issues and decisions confronting those who administer justice have an important economic component, and can be made the focus of analysis by economists. In this chapter we look at two such areas, the first being the question of whether judges represent, in one sense or other, a better means of deciding criminal cases than do juries and the second the question of how vigorously it is expedient for courts to pursue offenders who fail to pay fines that have been imposed on them.

In both cases we find ourselves forced to retreat slightly from the position taken in the previous chapter. Although we would still insist that decisions about the administration of justice cannot be sensibly taken in isolation from concerns about the volume of crime being committed or about sentencing policy, it is clear that in day-to-day decision-making, governments will not find it possible to explore fully all the consequences of each decision that is made. The danger of course is that if decision-making becomes too fractured, and takes insufficient account of decisions and costs elsewhere in the system, then serious deficiencies may arise even if decisions 'on the ground' seem to make sense. Looking at the administration of the criminal justice system in England and Wales, it is difficult to resist the suggestion that a closer scrutiny of some of the decision-making procedures would throw up some major internal inconsistencies.

The arguments of the preceding paragraphs revolve around two main assertions. The first is that there is no obvious economic theory of public agencies which can be applied in an effort to understand how the criminal justice system is administered. The second is that the desire to discuss administrative matters and procedures at the same time as decisions are being made about punishment and crime control strategies may have to be compromised somewhat if any progress is to be made towards discussing the administrative issues of the day. The next section, in which we discuss just two such issues is thus rather more pragmatic and conventional than one might ideally like it to be.

THE CHOICE BETWEEN JUDGES AND JURIES

We look first at the question of how accused parties are to be tried. The treatment is selective, for this is an area about which a great deal has been said in the past, albeit not in many cases by economists. In order to keep as sharp a focus as possible on the issues and to focus on a feature of the system that could be relatively easily changed if it were found desirable, the discussion will be framed around the question of whether trials are best heard by a judge or jury.

Very few cases are heard in which evidence to be presented is manifestly certain to result in conviction or acquittal. There will generally remain doubts about the truth or completeness of certain pieces of evidence. The decision about whether to convict or not will accordingly rely upon a balance of probabilities. The presumption of innocence that is generally made means that a court will convict only if it is reasonably confident that the evidence implicates the defendant. Once the decision has been made about whether to convict, a choice has to be made about the appropriate sentence. For simplicity, it is assumed here that these two questions are separable, and further discussion of sentencing is deferred.

Mistakes

There are two basic types of error that a court can make when deciding a case: it can convict someone who is innocent or acquit someone who is guilty. Such at least is true if we consider straightforward instances in which a single charge is being preferred. In more complex cases where multiple charges are concerned there may not be a simple dichotomy between conviction and acquittal.

As far as costs are concerned, there are two aspects of the decision to convict or acquit that are particularly significant. The first of these is the question of the extent of the costs entailed by making mistakes of various kinds and the second, taken up in the next section, is the question of the costs entailed in the decision-making process itself. We now consider the first of these two categories.

The costs resulting from the wrongful conviction of an innocent party are likely to depend upon two factors, namely the costs of the punishment imposed and in addition any general loss of confidence in the effectiveness of the system. The first of these components is most likely to depend in turn upon the type of punishment involved. Imprisonment imposes costs both upon the individual, who loses his liberty and the chance to earn an income and spend it upon consumption, and upon society at large. The latter occurs if and when there is a loss of output resulting from locking the person up. These costs falling upon the remainder of society rather than the person imprisoned will also include the resource costs of running prisons, which are well known to be high (Shaw, 1980). Once the prison term has been served, the resource loss is irrecoverable: the time and effort that the prisoner could have devoted to productive activities is lost for ever. Had the person been fined however, few unavoidable costs would have been incurred, irrespective of whether the mistake is ever discovered. This is of course because the fine represents a *redistribution* of resources rather than a real loss of resources as it does in the case of imprisonment. This may be of precious little consolation to the innocent party who has been fined, since he has paid his fine and the rest of society has appropriated some of the resources that he would otherwise have enjoyed himself. If the mistake is discovered, the fine can be repaid to the innocent person, whilst in any other event we can take some comfort from the thought that society gets some benefit from the revenue it has raised.

In addition to the resource costs entailed by mistakenly imprisoning an innocent party are the more general costs which may result in the event that the mistake comes to light. Empirically, rather few mistakes are discovered, and because it is virtually impossible to establish what number of mistakes remains undiscovered this may seem a rather fruitless area for discussion. Nevertheless, it is certainly possible to imagine circumstances in which mistakes may come to be a major source of concern. If it becomes known that mistakes are frequent, public confidence in the criminal justice system will decline and some of the deterrent impact of punishment may be lost. Any increase in the sense of insecurity experienced by citizens as a result of their coming to fear that they run an increased risk of being imprisoned for crimes they have not committed will represent a loss of aggregate happiness or social welfare.

In the opposite set of circumstances where guilty parties are being acquitted, the deterrent effect of punishment may again be undermined, since prospective criminals revise downwards their estimate of the probability of being convicted in the event that they choose to commit crime. Since wrongful acquittal entails no punishment being imposed, no direct resource costs will result from such errors. Returning for a moment to the question of how acquitting the guilty may weaken the deterrent value of punishment, it is useful to stress that it will be important to establish whether would-be criminals are able to determine for themselves the frequency with which the guilty are acquitted. If the error is not publicised by the fortunate criminal and it is not discovered publicly, then prospective criminals will have to make their own guess about whether the defendant was in fact guilty or not. This brings out into the open the fact that the *rate* of acquittals in a court may convey only *limited information* to would-be offenders. Without full knowledge of the details of different cases, it may be difficult for individuals to determine the likelihood that if they were caught they would be acquitted. Each case is examined by the court in some detail, and each will vary in several, possibly a great many, respects. To know, let us say, that the court acquits two defendants out of ten on average is not sufficient grounds to infer that the probability of a randomly-drawn defendant being acquitted is two in ten. Having said this however the would-be offender may well decide that the average acquittal rate constitutes the best guess that he can readily make about his own prospects in the event of being caught and put on trial.

The foregoing discussion of mistakes makes no mention of whether the likelihood that different sorts of mistakes are made will depend in any way upon whether the case is being tried by a judge or by a jury. Judges are professional decision-makers almost by definition, whilst jury members are strictly occasional. The question that suggests itself is whether a single judge (or a panel of three judges) is likely to make 'better' decisions than a jury composed of randomly-picked citizens. Two difficulties plague attempts to answer this question: first, how is it possible to establish the differences, if any, between the decisions that would be reached in any particular case and secondly, if differences can be established, what criterion is to be applied in discerning the 'better' decision? Suffice it to say that it is possible to do little more than speculate on such questions. The tentative suggestions that may be used as a starting point are first that statistical analysis of conviction and acquittal rates in cases decided by different means may give a guideline to the differences and secondly that a model of cost minimisation may be applied in reaching an assessment of which form of decision-making is best.

There are unfortunately, many possible objections to these suggestions. It is, for example, difficult to be sure that cases in which decisions are to be compared are actually comparable in all germane respects. Equally, it would be an elaborate exercise for a researcher to establish any idea of the various sorts of costs involved in even a single decision, so that attempts to verify the hypothesis that courts might, in their decisions, be attempting to minimise costs would simply not be feasible.

The inevitable conclusion seems to be that attempts to measure the quality of judicial decision-making relative to jury decision-making cannot at present be contemplated. Complete pessimism is however rarely helpful. In this instance, there are some lines of attack that are showing some limited promise. In one recent study (Baldwin and McConville 1979) an attempt was made to establish the quality of the decisions being made by juries in Birmingham. The authors, by interviewing the 'legal professionals' involved in cases which were heard by a jury, set out to establish the likelihood that judges, the prosecution and others would agree with the verdict reached by the jury. Their main finding was that there was evidence in many cases that the professionals would have reached the same verdict as the jury. For present purposes, this exercise is of limited help, since, considered in isolation, it does not shed light on whether any discrepancy between jury and professional opinion is greater or less than the discrepancy that would be found between judge-made decisions and professional opinion. If it is difficult to draw conclusions about the frequency of, and thus the costs associated with, the making of mistakes by different bodies, it is slightly easier to say something about the direct administrative costs of the different methods for reaching verdicts.

Administrative Costs

Ignoring the cost implications of any differences in the decisions that judges and juries make, we focus here on the running costs likely to be generated by each. To proceed thus is not to argue that qualitative differences in decision-making are irrelevant or that administrative costs are paramount: it is merely to point out that administrative costs may be different under the alternative decision-making regimes, and that discussion of which system is superior should not ignore such costs. A certain proportion of administrative costs will be unaffected by whether decisions are being made by judges or juries. The maintenance costs of court buildings, the salaries of full-time officials and many of the costs of record-keeping will all be incurred in either case. They can therefore be ignored here, although in a different context they may be a relevant matter. The main variable element will be the costs of judges' salaries, and wage-related costs such as subsistence, as compared with the costs of employing juries.

The temptation at this point is to argue that the costs of the two methods can be simply compared by assessing the amount of public expenditure on maintaining a judge for the duration of an average case and the amount of compensation for lost earnings claimed by an average jury over the course of an average case. This narrow view of costs ignores the fact that jury members are basically conscripts: they are obliged to do jury service if asked, and there is a low limit on the degree to which they may reclaim any lost wages. Many large companies and public employers do not stop paying their employees who are summoned to do jury service, and in such instances the courts may appear to get their jury members 'free'. However, as has been emphasised frequently in the course of this work, costs are to do with losses in the overall value of production, not with the amounts that particular individuals pay to others. The costs of employing someone to do jury service are measured by the opportunity cost of the person's time; what would have been their contribution to the value of output if they had continued their usual job rather than having time off to do jury service?

When looked at in this way, it becomes clear that the costs of juries may be in excess of the amounts recorded in the court's accounts showing the level of payments to jurors. In the case of jurors who claim nothing because their employer continues to pay their salary, the recorded figures understate the true cost by (approximately) the amount of the individual's pre-tax earnings. In other cases, jurors may claim for loss of earnings but find that the ceiling imposed on the amount that the court is allowed to pay is such as to leave them out of pocket. In these instances, the true costs of the juror's services are again equal to his pre-tax earnings, so that the extent of under-recording is equal to the difference between these earnings and the amount actually paid by the court.

Note that the true cost is in each case being met by someone. If the company keeps paying the employee's salary, the costs will be shared by the company's shareholders (who receive less profits) and by the consumers of the company's products (who pay higher prices). If a public authority continues paying an employee's salary, then the burden will fall on the tax payer. A self-employed individual on the other hand will face a loss if the income ceiling lies below his normal earnings, just as will an employee who finds his employer unwilling to continue paying his salary. Thus it is that the 'costs' of jury service may be met in part by the courts but in part also by a variety of employees, employers, consumers and shareholders: someone always pays! The degree of under-recording will depend upon the proportion of people doing jury service who continue to be paid by their employer and by the upper limit on the amount of earnings that can be reclaimed. In the UK at present, financial pressures are making employers in both the public and private sectors increasingly reluctant to subsidise jury service, whilst the ceiling on payments lies below the level of average earnings with the result that many costs are being absorbed by jurors themselves. At the time of writing (early 1982) the maximum that can be recovered for loss of earnings by a juror is £17 per day, or £85 per week. This figure should be compared with average earnings for men over 21, which are currently £142 per week, and the corresponding figure for women of £91 per week. As far as the juror himself is concerned, the relevant (private) calculation is to compare compensation for loss of earnings with *after-tax income,* but from the point of view of society at large, costs will be underestimated in the court's accounts by the difference between the ceiling on claims for loss of earnings and *pre-tax income.*

The net result of the undervaluing of the services of jurors is that the jury system is actually considerably more costly to maintain than might otherwise be thought. Whether or not juries are really more costly than the judiciary to maintain depends upon a variety of factors, including the relation between judges' salaries and industrial earnings, but in particular upon the number of judges who would be used in each case in the absence of a jury. Nowadays a judge is present in any case in jury trials, and if he were to be deprived of his jury and were to make the decision himself, then considerable savings could obviously be made. If however, a panel of three judges were to replace the one judge plus twelve jurors, the calculation would be a great deal finer, as I have argued elsewhere (Bowles, 1980).

Whilst the issue has thus far been cast as a comparison of the relative costs of using a judge (or judges) rather than a jury, others have gone further and argued that it may be possible to find ways of reducing the costs of juries. One suggestion, made by Tullock (1971), is that more specialist jurors could be used, thereby reducing the time taken by trials. Another suggestion, made by Martin (1972), is that costs could be reduced by making jury service voluntary rather than compulsory. The essence of their argument, which is developed in the context of an analogy with conscript armies, is that costs could be reduced by attracting to jury service those whose time would not otherwise be used in particularly valuable ways. Thus it would be that offering a wage for jury service, and adjusting the wage until one could attract the required number of jurors, would ensure that opportunity costs could be kept to a minimum. The drawback of such a system is of course that a jury would be self-selected rather than randomly-chosen. Whether in turn this would be sufficient grounds for rejecting such a solution (which in economic terms is rather attractive) would depend upon whether the degree of self-selection would be considerably higher than it is at present; upon whether the new juries would reach different decisions and upon the degree of political significance attaching to the use of randomly-selected juries, amongst other things. The resolution of such an issue lies beyond the scope of an economic analysis of the area, but such analysis has thrown up insights that more conventional discussion of the judge versus jury debate has overlooked. We move now from discussion of how trials are to be organised to a much less commonly debated area, namely the question of how court offices administer fines once they have been imposed.

THE ENFORCEMENT OF FINES

As suggested in the previous chapter, considerable variation exists in the way in which different courts administer fines. This variation marks the 'success' that different courts have in collecting the fines that they impose, the administrative devices that the courts use and finally the volume of resources that courts devote to collecting fines. To use a crude analogy with the theory of the firm, one could express these variations as characterising the pattern of inputs used by the firm, the technology used to transform inputs into outputs and the pattern of output itself. If one were to set out to produce a manual outlining 'best practice' it would be essential to recognise these three distinct components and to reach a view upon the 'correct' decisions in each case. As is so often true, sensible decisions in one area will both influence and be influenced by decisions in another: decisions about the appropriate number of court staff to assign to collecting fines are closely linked to decisions about whether collecting a high proportion of the fines imposed is accorded a higher or lower priority than other activities upon which court staff might be employed.

In order to keep the discussion as relevant as possible to the sorts of decisions being made by those who administer the criminal justice system, we identify three layers of decisions that have to be made, and discuss them in turn. The first decision concerns the objective that administrators take themselves to be pursuing, the second concerns decisions about day-to-day policy matters and the third concerns policy decisions made at a level somewhere between the first two.

Objectives

It seem natural, as an economist, to argue that the objective
of policy makers will be to find the combination of inputs
and outputs that will maximise social advantage. As in many
parts of the public sector this inclination can be difficult to
implement. Although the costs of collecting fines may be a
straightforward matter (at least in principle), how are the
benefits of collecting fines to be measured, or in what units
may 'output' be measured? The intuitively-appealing answer
is to measure output or benefits as the amount of revenue
collected, or possibly as the proportion of fines levied that is
successfully recovered. Having once done this, it is but a
short step to argue that the objective to be pursued is to
choose a pattern of enforcement activities that will maximise
the difference between the revenue collected and the costs
incurred. At this point, however we may shout STOP!

Whilst it is probably fair to say that many public agencies
concerned with revenue collection have a tendency, when
called upon to account for the quality of their activities, to
rely upon a comparison of their own operating costs with the
volume of revenue that they have collected, this is not to say
that such a comparison is relevant. Tax authorities are rather
similar to courts in this respect: the agency will claim that it
has collected £x million whilst only itself spending £y million.
A variant upon this measure of 'profit', and an apparently
more subtle one, is the claim for example, that some
proportion of tax evasion has been eliminated by the use of
more thorough enquiries, and that the extra cost of the
enquiries has been less than the extra revenue thus recovered.
In the case of court offices collecting fines the same sort of
argument is likely to appear in the guise of a claim that a
clamp-down on non-payers of fines has produced more
revenue than the exercise cost to mount. The question is: do
such calculations have any meaning?

The short answer is no. Fines, like taxes (and subsidies for
that matter) represent a *redistribution* of existing wealth: they
do not represent a creation or destruction of wealth in
themselves even though ultimately their existence may

influence incentives and thus the allocation of resources. The collection of fines on the other hand is an activity that absorbs resources in the form of buildings, officials' time and so on that could otherwise be used in productive ways. It follows that little is to be learnt from a comparison of the volume of revenue collected (or the proportion of revenue successfully collected) with the volume of costs incurred in the process of collection, for this is to fail to compare like with like. The benefits that result from successful collection of fine revenue are measured by the *reduction in the costs of crimes committed*. Thus if more successful collection of fines serves to deter some crimes, the degree of success is measured by the value of this deterrence effect. If some measure of 'profit' is required, it makes much more sense to compare the value of improved deterrence with the costs of increasing the proportion of revenue successfully than to compare the volume of revenue with the costs of collection.

This conclusion is depressing to the extent that measuring deterrent effects is a great deal more troublesome than measuring the amount (or proportion) of revenue collected. It does not however mean that the volume of revenue collected is somehow irrelevant. A considerable number of policy questions will require revenue information and not require any estimates of deterrence. If for example, different ways of organising the activities of court officials are being considered, it will be most relevant to ask which method of organisation will generate the greatest volume of revenue. The point in this instance is that the same costs of collection are entailed, but different amounts of revenue may result. In such cases it is legitimate to choose the method generating most revenue, since it may be assumed that this method will have the greatest impact on deterrence. It does not affect the argument to suggest that the effect may only be small in size.

Although the policy maker may be grateful that there are *some* questions that he can answer without investigating the deterrent value of successful fine collection, he should remember the limitations. It is well also to point out that even measuring the amount of revenue collected generates statistical problems that may be difficult for the policy maker to surmount. Should, for example, fines that are successfully recovered, but are not recovered within the time specified by the court at the time of sentence, be counted as genuine successes or not? A further difficulty is the likelihood that the fines imposed over some period by a court will be collected over a protracted interval. Some will be paid off immediately, but others will be around for a long time: the courts may lose track of an offender, but not declare the case 'dead' for some time in the hope that the offender will resurface. In the interim, much fine revenue imposed at different times will be received by the court office, and it may be insuperably complicated to identify the relevant payments. An attempt to measure in 1981, say, the proportion of fines imposed in 1979 and subsequently collected may be extremely difficult because:

(i) these fines were collected over 1979, 1980 and 1981, and some are still outstanding;
(ii) fines imposed in 1977 and 1978, and possibly earlier years also, enter the collection records for 1979 and 1980.

The result of (i) and (ii) is that any endeavour to match fines imposed with fines collected may produce curious results.

In England and Wales however the ratio of fine revenue collected to new fines imposed in each quarter seems to be taken quite seriously as an indicator of success, despite the problems just outlined. Any attack on the inadequacy of using such criteria should be tempered somewhat by recognition of the fact that under present arrangements information about variables other than those of revenue collected and fines imposed (that are in any event required for 'book-balancing' purposes) is virtually non-existent. In 1980, for example, a Parliamentary question (written number 65, 24 November 1980) was asked about the volume of fines outstanding and the costs being incurred in the course of the collection of fine revenue. The answer to the first part was given as approximately £30 million as at June 30 of that year. The answer to the second part was that: 'The costs of enforcing court orders are not distinguishable from other costs of the magistrates' courts and the police'. In the final analysis a properly designed information system is surely required that allows a more sophisticated means of monitoring and controlling events.

As far as 'top-level' decisions about how much to spend on collecting fines is concerned, the conclusion of this first section is that an efficient or optimal enforcement policy would require information that is not at present available, and that decisions based on the ad hoc indicators that *can* be constructed from existing data may be inefficient and ill-conceived. The next question is whether one need be so pessimistic about the quality of day-to-day decisions made by court enforcement agencies.

Day-to-day decisions.

The justices' clerk, who at the local level takes responsibility for day-to-day decision-making by his court staff, has to ensure that sensible practices are followed in enforcing fines. A close look at what goes on behind the scenes reveals that courts differ widely in the formal and informal tactics they use against offenders who fail to pay their fines on time. In some courts, even quite junior staff exercise considerable discretion over the rate of payment that will be accepted in instances where offenders claim to be unable to meet the obligations imposed upon them at sentence. Elsewhere, legal proceedings may be taken as a matter of routine against offenders who miss one or two payments. When action is taken, the court staff have a range of options. Some, such as the issue of distress warrants (under which some of the offender's possessions are confiscated) are rarely used. Others, such as reminder letters or the issue of a means warrant (requiring the offender to appear before the court and to explain why he has failed to pay) are much more widely used.

Several observations may be made upon such decision-taking. In the first place, little if anything seems to be known about the relative costs of using these different tactics. It is perhaps fair to add that this does not mean that there are no incentives for efficient use of available resources. The staff may be quite aware that some of the procedures are more time-consuming than others and that some of the procedures are more likely to result in payment than others. The desires of individual staff to either minimise the efforts they have to make to do the job reasonably or to achieve promotion by means of bringing about improvements in recovery rates may both tend to encourage a sensible use of manpower. Staff on the other hand, are not paid directly on a results basis and promotion prospects may not be particularly sensitive to whether recovery rates are rising or falling.

The other difficulty that plagues the incentive argument is one that pervades many types of public office. There may be some procedures that involve other agencies and thus seem rather attractive to court staff. The obvious example is police involvement. Both reminder letters and notices to appear before a means enquiry may be issued either by the court or by the police, and yet in many instances it is the police who do the job. Although it is generally claimed by court staff that fine defaulters are more likely to respond to police actions than to actions by court officials, the cynic might be tempted to suggest that court staff rely on police help because it reduces the costs falling on the court. Whether the job is best done by court officials or the police depends upon the salaries of the staff doing the job in each case and on the speed with which they can do it. The point of the argument is not that court staff ought to be doing this task, merely that they have an incentive to pass the job on to somebody else!

It can then be seen that the familiar arguments about incentives and costs arise just as much in the day-to-day operation of a court office as in higher level discussions of the structure of the criminal justice system. It is perhaps also worth reiterating that there are many decisions that are still regarded as matters of purely administrative or judicial concern that have quite serious consequences for resource use. To ignore these consequences is to ignore the fact that resources used by the criminal justice system could normally be used for other purposes, and is to treat the search for justice as being an absolute goal that must be pursued at the expense of all others.

Intermediate decisions

Between the decision-making levels discussed in the previous two sub-sections lies a decision-making body that has significant responsibility for resource use. The Magistrates' Courts' Committee is responsible for the magistrates' courts in a county or county borough. Its membership is drawn exclusively from magistrates who sit in the county, although its meetings are generally attended by invited members of the local authority. It is this Committee which, inter alia, considers requests from the clerk to a local magistrates' court for extra resources. It is important to note at this point that magistrates courts are financed 80 per cent by a grant from the Home Office (that is from central government) and 20 per cent by the local authority.

For various, fairly obvious, reasons it is desirable that the judiciary are independent of government control. It is quite another matter however to argue that magistrates should play as prominent a part as they do in making decisions about the use of resources by courts. Although under the present system the local authority (who are immeditely responsible for paying bills before reclaiming their 80 per cent grant from the Home Office) can object to increases in resources that are decided by the Magistrates' Courts' Committee, it is clear that resource decisions are effectively being made by those who work within the system rather than by those who are financing it. It would be churlish to describe magistrates as anything other than responsible and capable, but at the same time it would be rather presumptuous to expect them to be particularly expert at managing large budgets.

The distinctive feature of intermediate level decisions can thus be thought of as being the isolation of those making decisions from the relevant financial pressures, although in practice they are apparently sensitive to local authority views in a rather general way. In addition to this isolation however are many of the problems arising at other decision-making levels: little seems to be known about whether expanding the staffing of local courts will have much effect on the proportion of fines collected, for example, and rather less seems to be known about whether more vigorous enforcement of fines can be expected to influence crime rates and thus the cost of crime.

SUMMARY AND CONCLUSIONS

The main object of this chapter has been to pursue the suggestion, made in earlier chapters on the criminal justice system, that the administration of justice is ideally to be thought of as an integral part of a model of crime and punishment. The advantage that such an approach has is that it enables the relation between different parts of the criminal justice system to be clearly recognised and allows for a coherence of treatment that is missed by most other approaches. In practice however it seems to be clear that justice is not administered in a way that is conducive to the achievement of this ideal. The two areas explored in this chapter illustrate this contention, but they are only intended as examples. The same kinds of argument can be applied to many other administrative matters of law and order. Thus whilst it may be naive to imagine constructing an economic model of the criminal justice system which would enable decisions about expenditure on crime prevention, on the enforcement of punishment and so on to be made simultaneously, there are at least some rather more piecemeal steps that can be suggested in the light of economic arguments.

This chapter has only touched on the great variety of issues posed by the criminal justice system, and has perforce been highly selective. The first part, concerned with the choice between judges and juries as the 'best' decision-making agency in criminal trials, exploited the idea of the jury member as an involuntary worker and suggested that unless a very high value is put on the jury being conscripted on some sort of random basis, it might be useful to at least consider the idea of making jury service a voluntary, paid job like any other. The second part took up the question of how decisions about fine enforcement are, and might be, made. It was suggested that at present in England and Wales, decisions about fine enforcement policy are made at different levels, but that in no case does there seem to be an attempt to establish a systematic framework for either discussing or informing policy questions.

Various other aspects of the system have been looked at by economists, but many others seem as yet to have avoided such a fate. Amongst the studies of which no mention has been made is the work by Landes (1971) which looks at the question of how a public prosecutor, faced by limitations on the amount of court time and the budget for legal services that he has at his disposal, assigns his scarce resources amongst the cases that he would like to bring. It is to be hoped that more economists will interest themselves in the future in these kinds of issues because until then it will remain difficult to persuade the sceptic that interesting conclusions can be drawn from an application of economic analysis to this traditionally 'soft' area.

FURTHER READING

The administrative issues thrown up in the course of operating the criminal justice system would seem to be a natural concern for economists. Relatively little work has however been done in this area. Noteworthy exceptions are work by Landes (1971) on the administration of courts, Landes (1973) on the bail system, Martin (1972) on the conscription of juries and, more recently, Shaw (1980) on the costs of various penal sanctions.

7

Tort

THE OBJECTIVES OF THE TORT SYSTEM

Tort law over the last two decades has figured prominently in the writings of a number of economists. It has for the most part been welcomed as a most useful device and one that is in many respects superior to its main rivals, principally statutory provision. Claims about this absolute and relative superiority are generally based upon the ability of a system of tort law to enable market-like transactions and negotiation between agents, that might otherwise be inhibited, to take place. Many of the major activities to which tort law applies entail potential conflict between individuals: tort law provides a framework enabling the resolution of such conflict. The creation of a series of enforceable rights and obligations enables parties to know the terms under which they can engage in many of the activities where they stand to suffer damage as a result of the behaviour of others.

From an economic point of view the object of having an effective system of property rights (as the bundle of rights and obligations is normally termed) is to create a device for ensuring that when individuals take actions which will impose costs upon others, those incurring the costs are able to recover compensation from, or to exercise some other remedy against those who are creating the costs. It should be remembered throughout this discussion that the object is not to eliminate all those actions or activities from which harm to person or property may result, but to try to ensure that they are eliminated if and only if the harm to which they give rise exceeds the gain. There are of course many difficulties that beset the achievement of this demanding objective whether tort law or some other institution is being used. This, as we show in the section on the current debate about whether social security provision should replace tort as the mechanism by which victims of road and other accidents recover compensation can lead to great controversy. Whether the tort system is really superior as many (but by no means all) economists would claim will depend upon quite fine judgments about the inadequacies of the tort system in relation to the imperfections of the alternatives.

The tort system can be thought of as a method for meeting two quite distinct sorts of aims, both of which are alluded to in the previous paragraph. In the first place, it can be used as a device to control the extent to which people engage in activities which potentially impose costs on others. This *deterrence* role is the one upon which much of the work of economists is concentrated. The tort system is compared with other methods of achieving the 'optimal' degree of deterrence such as the imposition of taxes on dangerous activities or the use of the criminal law in prohibiting or directly controlling them. The test of the efficacy of the tort system is thus a matter of establishing whether the pattern of activity under a tax or regulatory system lies closer to the pattern which would be associated with an efficient allocation of resources than the pattern generated under tort. To put it more bluntly, one would be concerned to establish whether the 'right' number of victims is created under tort, given the costs incurred by victims and the benefits generated by the activity in question.

The second function or role of the tort system is to enable victims of tort to recover *compensation*. The distinctive feature of tort in this respect is that the compensation will generally be recoverable, if at all, from a person to whose actions the harm may be attributed. The 'quality' of the tort system in this second respect will be a matter of establishing the degree to which victims are able to recover amounts of damages that adequately reflect their losses and whether the degree to which the tort system achieves such an end is greater or lesser than the degree enabled under alternative schemes.

On the deterrence view, the prime objective of tort law is to

ensure that participants in a great range of activities are
confronted by a bundle of incentives and disincentives which
is consistent with the derivation of the greatest possible net
social advantage from activities taken both individually and
as a whole. If an individual's actions might impose harm on
others then, roughly speaking, we will wish to ensure that he
takes full account of these costs when deciding whether, or
how vigorously, to pursue such actions. Tort law may thus
play an important role in creating channels via which
appropriate cost pressures can be transmitted to those
making decisions that have potentially harmful effects. The
cost pressures should be neither exaggerated nor understated,
since either kind of deviation will militate against resources
being used in the most valuable possible way.

This basic argument may be applied in many different
settings. The speed at which motorists drive will influence
both the benefits from driving, since it affects journey time,
and also the costs which are created in the form of danger to
other road users. The object is to encourage drivers to choose
a speed which fully reflects the relative size of these costs and
benefits: losses will result if motorists are encouraged to drive
too quickly or too slowly. There is nothing novel about this
argument, and it seems to be as well established in law as it is
in the work of economists. In *Daborn v. Bath Tramways
Motor Company Ltd* [1946] for example, Lord Justice
Asquith, in a case concerning the style in which an ambulance
was driven, said that: 'As has often been pointed out, if all
the trains in the country were restricted to a speed of five
miles an hour, there would be fewer accidents, but our
national life would be intolerably slowed down'. The
argument applies equally well in the case of employers
deciding how elaborate should be the precautions to
safeguard workers. 'Excess' provision of safety precautions
would mean higher production costs and thus a higher
product price, less production and fewer workers taken on.
Equally, inadequate precautions will mean that very high
costs are being imposed on workers who suffer more
accidents; costs which are not justified in terms of the savings
to consumers or the higher level of employment.

Whilst economists have made much of the efficiency issue in their discussion of tort, they have tended to put much less emphasis on the distribution side of the question. It is quite clear from public debate of the matter however that people take very seriously the degree to which the tort system adequately compensates injured parties. In practice, tort operates alongside other institutions and the overall package is expected to fulfil a range of deterrence and compensatory functions as should become clear when we return to these issues in the discussion of the Report of the Royal Commission on Civil Liability.

<h2 style="text-align:center">EFFICIENCY, TRANSACTIONS COSTS AND THE ASSIGNMENT OF LIABILITY</h2>

The basic approach taken by the economist is the same irrespective of the category of tort involved. Thus although we rely heavily upon the example of accidents in this chapter the basic principles would be the same if applied to other areas of tort. The kinds of costs and benefits entailed will vary as between different categories. In some classes of tort the harm at issue may be serious physical injury or death whilst in others it may simply be inconvenience or loss of income. As well as there being different kinds of costs, there will also be different liability rules governing the conditions under which various kinds of remedies are available. Under a rule of strict liability for example the circumstances under which a person will be held responsible for compensating those harmed by his action or inaction will be much wider than those under which he would be held responsible if the damaged party has to demonstrate negligence or failure on the part of the defendant to meet some required standard of care. The economic analysis however is not fundamentally different.

The starting point is the famous article by Coase (1960) on 'The Problem of Social Cost'. In that lengthy and difficult paper the central argument is that the assignment of liability for damage will, in the final analysis, have no influence over how resources are allocated, *provided that transactions costs are zero.* As we outlined in chapter 2, private bargaining between parties can be relied upon to ensure that the best balance between their activities will be reached. This solution requires only two things: first, that some preliminary set of rules (or rights and obligations) be announced around which parties may bargain and secondly, that these rights and obligations can be shifted between the parties costlessly. The function of tort law when such conditions are met is simply to ensure the enforceability of the new allocation of rights agreed by the parties.

The difficulty of course is that in a great many situations in everyday life it is simply not plausible to assume that bargaining costs are negligible. Any theory which is based upon such a presumption, although it may be a useful starting point for a better theory, is unlikely to be of much intrinsic value. The Coase Theorem relies, for its conclusion about the unimportance attaching to the initial assignment of rights, on the assumption of zero bargaining costs, so that the observation that such costs do exist can be taken to imply that the initial assignment of rights *does* matter.

This assertion may be explained by reference to one of the favourite illustrations of the Coase Theorem in which a railroad runs across a farmer's land and sparks emitted by trains sometimes damage the farmer's crops. If costs of negotiating are negligible, it does not matter whether the farmer or the railroad is initially held responsible for the damage, since the parties will always come to an agreement over how often trains are to run, about whether sparkguards are to be fitted and about how near the railroad the farmer is to plant crops. Negotiation would result in the overall costs of fire damage and fire prevention activities being minimised, a solution which will be the same irrespective of the initial assignment of responsibility for damage. But if costs of negotiation should become significant and it thus becomes expensive for the parties to shift responsibility for damage between one another in the search for cost-reducing patterns of activity, then the final result may depend heavily upon the initial assignment of liability. It may be prohibitively expensive, that is to say, for the parties to lift themselves out of an initial position where there is an inefficient assignment of liability. If the gains from eliminating the inefficiency are smaller than the bargaining costs associated with such a move, the inefficiency persists and benefits that would be available from some other configuration of rules are foregone.

The existence of significant bargaining costs is much more likely if the railroad crosses the land of a great many individual farmers. If negotiation is to take place, a large number of individual deals will have to be made, and it is this which is likely to be a problem rather than the costs of negotiation between the railroad and an individual farmer. That is to say that if the initial assignment of rights takes a form which obviates the need for widespread negotiation, then overall costs may be lower than otherwise, and the final assignment of liability may conform more closely to the efficient pattern of assignment that would emerge if bargaining were costless.

The question that now emerges is how this initial assignment of rights is to be decided. Some method will have to be found for identifying which is the 'best' way of assigning liability in the event that the parties find themselves locked into the initial assignment because of high bargaining costs. Consider for example the case of the motorist and the pedestrian. Cars can very easily inflict heavy damage on pedestrians. Responsibility for such damage can be assigned initially to either group, but clearly there is little scope for the parties to bargain themselves into some superior position once the rule has been announced.

In such circumstances a decision has to be made about whether pedestrians themselves are to be liable for any accident they may meet, whether motorists are to be liable, whether both parties are to be given a duty to take care and so on. To emphasise the point made earlier, the choice between these assignments, if it is costly for the parties to escape an assignment once made, will determine the way in which both motorists and pedestrians behave and will thus influence the number of accidents involving pedestrians. The principle advocated by economists in such a context is that of assigning liability to the cheapest cost avoider. In the event that one or other of the parties can unambiguously be said to be able to reduce a risk at lower cost to himself than could the other party, he is the party upon whom liability should be imposed.

If motorists were always in a better position to anticipate accidents than pedestrians then it would be wise always to make motorists responsible. There are however many instances in which a trivial change in the behaviour of pedestrians may reduce accident risks very considerably. In many such instances to make motorists responsible would be to require motorists to drive a lot more carefully. The costs imposed upon motorists in this way may considerably exceed the costs at which pedestrians could take similarly-effective evasive action. Some accidents will still occur, since even if liability is assigned to the cheapest cost avoider there will continue to be occasions upon which the gains from a hazardous action will outweigh the likely costs.

Generally speaking, there will be some circumstances under which one group or party will have an advantage in the costs at which he can reduce risks and other circumstances where the reverse is true. In accident law for example motorists are generally held liable for certain sorts of accidents and pedestrians for others. It costs pedestrians little to cross roads sensibly rather than randomly or carelessly, and it would be wrong therefore to make motorists liable in instances where pedestrians are 'needlessly' creating accidents. Equally, motorists can quite cheaply anticipate various hazardous pedestrian practices, such as their failing to look over their shoulders before crossing a minor road where it intersects a main road. In such circumstances it is better to make motorists liable, since to slow down and check for pedestrians in such circumstances is not often a major inconvenience. This leads very naturally into a discussion of negligence and the way in which liability is assigned in practice.

NEGLIGENCE

Under English law the tort system is based on the notion of negligence, the principles of which were set out in a Scottish case, *Donoghue v. Stevenson* [1932]. In order for a party to succeed in recovering damages for negligence, a test comprising three elements has to be satisfied. It has to be shown by the plaintiff that (1) the defendant owed him a duty of care, (2) that the defendant, in breach of the duty, behaved negligently and (3) that damage to the plaintiff resulted from this breach. The first and third of these criteria are, at least from an economic point of view, straightforward. The first entails establishing the relevant property rights in the context of the damage at issue, whilst the third is directed at properly identifying whether the harm that has occurred may be attributed to the defendant's actions. Much more problematic is the second.

Almost all activities can be pursued more or less carefully and the likelihood of injury to oneself or others resulting will generally depend upon the degree of care which is exercised, as we have already stressed. To have established that a duty of care is owed is one thing but to show that the degree of care exercised in the event was sufficiently low as to constitute negligence is another. The difficulty is to identify the critical degree of care below which an action will be called negligent in the event of it giving rise to damage.

The degree of care judged to be appropriate in some particular instance may be deduced by asking questions about how a 'reasonable man' would have acted, or about whether an act was in some other respect 'reasonable'. Negligence might thus seem to be indicated when it can be shown that a defendant proceeded with an action that the hypothetical person would have realised was unreasonable. Atiyah (1980) however argues that a better guide to the decisions that judges make derives from thinking in terms of whether an action is 'desirable in the public interest'.

In either event one *could* argue that the law is groping towards the kind of test of negligence that an economist would propose. Such an 'economic test' could be posed in the following way: 'an action is said to be negligent if the benefits which derive from it are outweighed by the costs which, on average it is likely to generate'. This test can be readily illustrated as in figure 7.1. In this diagram, care is defined in terms of a percentage: zero care means that no thought at all is given to the consequences of the action, whilst if 100 per cent care is exercised, there are no remaining costs which could possibly result from the action that can be eliminated.

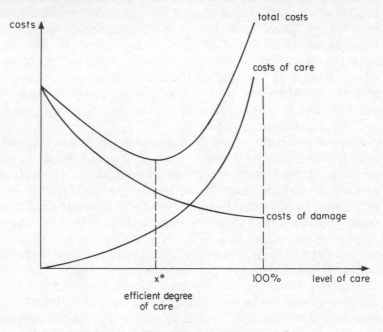

Figure 7.1 The Efficient Degree of Care

Taking greater care gives rise to higher costs, as indicated by the costs of care schedule, but also results in less harm occurring on average. Note that the average damage associated with a given degree of care may comprise an occasional catastrophe, or frequent minor costs. The *efficient level of care,* x^*, in the diagram occurs where the sum of the cost schedules, or total costs, is at a minimum. If less care is exercised the action is said to be negligent because it generates more costs than benefits. If more care is exercised, accidents will still occur occasionally, but the action is not negligent because it entails a degree of care that on average is socially beneficial.

This 'economic test' of negligence may seem to be a long way from the kinds of criteria actually used in English courts although, as we will suggest in a moment, it may not be quite as different as is sometimes argued. Even if one were to concede that English practice may not be readily rationalised by appeal to such a principle there are striking similarities between the 'economic test' and the so-called Learned Hand formula widely referred to in American writings. Hand was a judge in the United States who in a number of cases in the 1930s and 40s put forward guidelines for determining whether a defendant was to be held liable. Hirsch (1979) describes the formula in the following way:

Judge Learned Hand [..] defined the legal standard of liability applicable to most unintended acts of negligence as follows: the defendant is guilty of negligence if the loss caused by the event, for example, an accident, L, multiplied by the probability of the event occurring, P, exceeds the costs of the precautions that the defendants might have taken to avert it, C.

The main difference between the Hand formula and the economic test seems to be that the benefits of the activity are ignored in Hand's formulation. This is something of an illusion however, and the conflict may be resolved by thinking about the nature of what we mean by 'cost' in this context. The costs of preventing the damage in question will, at least in part, depend upon the benefits from the action. Provided that this is recognised, there is no real conflict between the Hand formula and the other test.

In order to illustrate how the approach works, let us take the case of the ambulance driver who is tempted to drive more quickly than usual in an effort to save the life of someone who has been severely injured. The benefits resulting from driving more quickly are the improved survival prospects of the patient, whilst the costs include an increased likelihood of having an accident. Suppose that the driver is contemplating raising his speed from 30 to 40 miles per hour, and that as a result the probability that he will have an accident in the course of his journey to the hospital rises from one in ten to one in eight. The minutes saved on the journey time would improve the survival chances of the patient, a gain upon which we choose to place a value of £5,000. In the event of an accident the patient will almost certainly die, the ambulance driver and other road users will be injured and the ambulance and other vehicles damaged, at a total cost of, say, £100,000. Leaving aside the possibility that many impetuous citizens would, in these circumstances, have no hesitation in driving off at top speed, what conclusions will we reach about whether, in the event of an accident occurring, the ambulance driver (or his employers) should be found negligent?

It seems quite clear that to drive at 40 miles per hour in these circumstances should not be regarded as negligent since the gains from doing so are valued at £5,000 compared with prospective damage costs of £2,500. The latter figure is the product of the increased probability of having an accident and the costs of such an accident. The change in costs and benefits associated with a higher speed may be summarised as:

$$
\begin{array}{lll}
\text{Value of raising speed} & = & \text{rise in benefits} - \text{rise in costs}
\end{array}
$$

$$
= \begin{array}{c}\text{improved} \\ \text{patient} \\ \text{survival} \\ \text{prospects}\end{array} - \begin{array}{c}\text{increased} \\ \text{probability} \\ \text{of an} \\ \text{accident}\end{array} \times \begin{array}{c}\text{cost} \\ \text{entailed} \\ \text{by an} \\ \text{accident}\end{array}
$$

$$
= +5,000 - (0.125 - 0.1) \times 100,000
$$

$$
= +5,000 - 2,500 = 2,500
$$

Since the benefits, on balance, exceed the costs the increased speed is justified. Suppose however that the driver considering raising his speed is not an ambulanceman but a casual motorist travelling to see friends at the weekend. The driver knows that driving at 40 miles per hour through the town rather than 30 miles per hour will save him five minutes on the journey time, a saving of little consequence, valued for the sake of argument at five pounds. We may suppose that such a policy would have the same effect on the risk of having an accident (namely increasing it from one in ten to one in eight), even though the accident may be less catastrophic, and cost only, say, £20,000. When we come to apply the same formula for evaluating an increase in speed we find this time that the figures are:

$$\text{value of raising speed} = \text{rise in benefits} - \text{rise in costs}$$
$$= +5 - \frac{1}{40} \cdot 20,000 = -495$$

The casual motorist is not therefore justified in raising his speed, since the net value of such a change would be negative.

There is an interesting example which is suggestive of the relevance of the circumstances in which an action takes place to the decision about whether the action was negligent. During the Second World War the driver of a left-hand drive ambulance had turned into a lane on the offside of the road without signalling. Lord Justice Asquith in *Daborn v. Bath Tramways* [1946] concluded that the ambulance driver had not broken her duty of care. In his speech he argued that:

In determining whether a party is negligent, the standard of reasonable care is that which is reasonably to be demanded in the circumstances. A relevant circumstance to take into account may be the importance of the end to be served by behaving in this way or that. During the war, it was necessary for many highly important operations to be carried out by means of motor vehicles with left-hand drives, no others being available. So far as this was the case, it was impossible for the drivers of such cars to give the warning signals which could otherwise be properly demanded of them . .
It seems to me, in those circumstances, it would be demanding too high and an unreasonable standard of care from the drivers of such cars to say to them: "Either you must give signals which the structure of your vehicle renders impossible or you must not drive at all".

For all that it is possible to adduce remarks by judges that are consistent with the economic model, it is very easy also to find academic writers and judges prepared to condemn an explicit arithmetical calculation. Atiyah (1980), for example, takes the view that

. . . any attempt to reduce the whole law of negligence to the form of an algebraic equation must be dismissed because we are not dealing with precisely measurable values.

In order for a Hand-type formula to be applied estimates have to be made of benefits that may include the value of human life and limb. Estimates have also to be made not only of the probability that accidents will occur, but also of changes in probabilities that are associated with variations in behaviour: how much *more* dangerous is it to drive at 40 miles per hour than at 30 miles per hour for example. Particularly if tort is to act as a sophisticated tool for expressing deterrence powers, it is important that judges can find principles and guidelines which make it possible for people to predict the circumstances in which negligence will be identified and the size of damage awards which will be made. It is important for the same reason that individuals have well-developed capacities for dealing with information about risks of different kinds and their consequences. The evidence about whether individuals are very good at assembling relevant information and making sensible calculations is not very encouraging. For a discussion of the difficulties of getting individuals to answer questions from which their attitudes towards the risk of death or serious injury may be inferred, see Jones-Lee (1976). We discuss elsewhere in this book some of the difficulties associated with valuing life and limb, and future income streams, as well as the likelihood that the procedures under which victims can press claims for damages for personal injury are likely to result in significant 'under-compensation'. We move now to examine some of the recent controversy that has sprung up over whether the tort system should be abolished as the major device through which victims of accidents seek damages.

ACCIDENTS, THE TORT SYSTEM AND PROPOSALS
FOR REFORM

This chapter has so far avoided the question of whether the
tort system as it operates in practice is seen to be smoothly
performing the allocative function which has been assigned to
it. The doubts expressed by Atiyah over the degree to which it
is possible to measure the appropriate costs and probabilities
raise one question mark and the structure of insurance
policies under which participants in hazardous activities
protect themselves from the costs of causing damage raises
another. These concerns have prompted various proposals
for reform. In the following sections we look first at the
relation between tort and the institution of private insurance
and secondly at the effects that proposals to abolish tort
might have upon the allocation and distribution of resources
in those areas of accidental damage in which tort actions are
currently available.

Tort and Insurance

One of the central problems arising from use of the tort
system for accident compensation is that the costs of many
accidents are simply beyond the pocket of those involved.
Serious personal injuries may have a catastrophic effect on an
individual's lifetime earnings, and in most cases it is
unimaginable that the tortfeasor could himself assume
responsibility for paying an appropriate sum as
compensation. This will at least be true when we are thinking
of individuals or small firms. Larger firms, such as
pharmaceutical firms or airlines, incurring major damage
claims may have sufficient funds or borrowing power to meet
claims. But for the most part, parties will have to take out
insurance if they are to avoid bankrupting themselves.
Indeed, so serious is this problem in the context of motoring
that the government makes it compulsory for drivers to have
a valid third party insurance policy which will ensure that any
victim of their negligence has a chance of recovering
something by way of compensation.

The reliance upon a compulsory insurance scheme to avoid

the problem of bankruptcy unfortunately has some undesirable consequences. If a driver's liability for causing damage is taken over by his insurance company he is no longer directly responsible himself for meeting the costs that his carelessness is imposing on others. In the extreme case, the insurance company meets the entire cost of any claim, so that whilst the victim may be compensated, the insured person only suffers to the extent that his accident has caused himself suffering as well. In the case of motorists injuring pedestrians for example, although the driver may incur some degree of mental distress at running someone over, it is unlikely that he will incur much injury or damage himself.

This 'moral hazard' effect of insurance as it is called occurs in an even more extreme guise under comprehensive insurance cover. A driver who is insured against the costs of any damage to himself that is not the fault of a third party is effectively avoiding all possible costs that his negligence may generate. In such circumstances, the individual's incentives to exercise care may be very slight and may disappear altogether.

This argument may be illustrated by a simple adaptation of figure 7.1. In the event of the driver being fully insured, he is fully insulated from the costs of any damage he may cause, whilst in the absence of any insurance, he is fully liable for damage up to the level of negligent care, but exempt beyond it. If, for simplicity we ignore the possibility that some of the damage his negligence causes may affect himself, we can readily establish the impact that introducing insurance will have. In figure 7.2 if the individual carries no insurance then his costs will be the same as in figure 7.1, costs indicated by the schedule TC_1. After insuring himself however the individual perceives his total cost schedule to have moved to TC_2 where the liability for paying damages has been completely removed. In this rather extreme form of the argument it can be seen that the individual's choice of the degree of care will move from x^* without insurance to zero when he becomes fully insured. The only costs he now incurs are the cost of the insurance policy, i, which for convenience are omitted from the diagram.

Thus, paradoxically, the institution of compulsory insurance, designed to ensure that drivers are able to meet the costs of successful claims against them, may have the effect of greatly diminishing the deterrent value of the tort system.

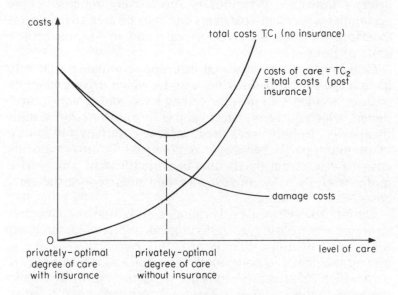

Figure 7.2 The Effects of Insurance on the Optimal Degree of Care

Insurance companies will however have strong incentives to try and prevent carelessness amongst the drivers they insure and the resulting measures that they take may offset some of the undermining effects of insurance. The basic strategy that insurance companies use in their efforts to encourage drivers to exercise more care is to search for ways in which the size of the premium that a driver pays can be made to reflect the degree of care the driver shows. The most popular indicators used in efforts to discriminate amongst more and less careful drivers are previous accident record, any record of convictions for traffic offences, type of car driven and driver's occupation. In diagrammatical terms, this may be interpreted as an effort to change the total cost schedule as it is perceived by drivers. By shifting perceived costs from the schedule TC_2 as in figure 7.2 back to a position such as TC_1, the insurance company may be able to persuade the driver to exercise the degree of care which is optimal for society. Devices such as the 'no claims bonus' system under which a driver's insurance premium is successively reduced as he accumulates accident-free years can thus be seen to be central to efforts to maintain levels of care and to keep down the costs of insurance.

Other methods upon which insurance companies may rely include the use of 'deductibles', under which drivers meet the costs of accidents up to some ceiling level, and 'co-insurance' under which drivers meet some proportion of claims themselves. In both cases the insurance company will reduce its premium partly because it is now passing on some of its costs to drivers but partly also because the driver may drive more carefully as a consequence and thus reduce the total costs he is generating.

Despite such measures, it remains clear that the incentive structure confronting an individual driver is a rather blunt tool, and something that is probably not very effective at getting the driver to continually monitor and adjust the care with which he drives. Serious accidents are relatively rare in the sense that a reasonably careful driver can expect to drive for a long time before he has one. To induce people to take the appropriate degree of care in the face of occasional catastrophe is likely to be much more difficult than in the face of regular minor accidents like being caught in the rain without a coat. This argument applies with greater impact if a compulsory insurance policy removes many of the costs of a catastrophe from the careless party.

Amongst the devices that are used alongside the tort system to help persuade drivers to take appropriate precautions, are various provisions that would almost certainly be retained, and possibly strengthened, if the tort system were no longer to be used in the accident sphere. Liability to prosecution under the criminal law for offences ranging from causing death by dangerous driving, manslaughter through dangerous and careless driving, driving while unfit and driving with excess speed are all ways of encouraging drivers to exercise greater care. Equally, there are requirements relating to the driver's competence. Age or failure to pass the driving test may preclude an individual from driving at all or from driving whilst unaccompanied. Requirements relating to the mechanical fitness of vehicles are another channel through which pressure to reduce accidents may be channelled.

Tort versus Social Insurance

When it comes to reviewing the effectiveness of tort, it is important to be able to identify the source of the incentives to take care which drivers confront. If these incentives derive largely from the existence of the tort action then abolishing tort will probably raise accident rates. If on the other hand the incentives can be shown to derive principally from the institution of criminal liability or some other source which would most probably be maintained even if tort were discontinued then accident rates may not be very much affected. It is of course very difficult to establish empirically whether accident rates would change significantly if the basis for the compensation of accident victims were switched from a system of civil liability to a no-fault system under which compensation was paid from a social security type fund.

The recent debate in England over whether a no-fault scheme such as the one used in New Zealand should be introduced has had to confront precisely the issue of whether any efficiency losses from the abolition of tort would be offset by improvements in the degree to which victims are adequately compensated. This debate has not however thrown up much evidence on the question of the likely effects of a change in the method of compensation on accident rates. It has nonetheless created a great amount of documentary evidence of the degree to which, under present arrangements, many victims fail to recover damages. From the research conducted by the Royal Commission on Civil Liability (the Pearson Commission: Royal Commission, 1978) and the large-scale survey conducted by the Centre for Socio-Legal Studies in Oxford, it has become clear that many accident victims fail to recover anything like the amount of compensation for their injuries that would be required to satisfy the criterion of returning them (insofar as money is able) to the position that they would have been in had the accident not occurred.

The superiority of the social security system is argued by its advocates to derive from two factors. The first is that the pattern of compensation payments made under a social insurance approach will be more finely tuned to the needs of accident victims, if only because many of the obstacles confronting those seeking compensation under tort would disappear. The second factor is the likelihood that the costs of distributing a given sum of compensation to accident victims will be lower than those generated by the tort system. This argument is based on the observation that the costs of administering existing social security funds are very much lower per pound of benefit distributed than the corresponding costs of distributing damages recovered under tort. These latter costs are high because of the very high costs of legal resources used in efforts to establish liability and quantum.

In reality of course the abolition of tort would hardly be a panacea for accident victims. It is likely that some victims who currently are seriously undercompensated would do better, but the move would be from one mixed system (tort and its complements) to another mixed system (social insurance and its complements). The net allocative effects would depend upon how the new system was financed and upon whether incentives to take care were preserved. As the comments of Professor Prest in the Pearson Commission Report emphasize, it is important not to lose sight of the quest for efficiency in trying to achieve justice.

CONCLUDING REMARKS

The proponents of the tort system regard it as a flexible and subtle device that permits society to enjoy higher levels of wealth than are otherwise possible. It is seen as an important complement to the market mechanism and as something which has many market-like characteristics. This school often advocates that many activities which are currently regulated by statutory provision and by government agencies would benefit from being opened up to the pressures that tort would bring.

Critics of tort on the other hand take the view that there are many problems associated with tort that prevent the emergence of solutions that are demonstrably superior in terms of allocative efficiency and/or of their distributive consequences. The difficulties experienced by those suffering damage in successfully recovering compensation from tortfeasors and the high costs of legal services combine to inhibit effective use of the tort action. In the case of accidents, it is argued that the existence of insurance may seriously weaken incentives and at the same time involve costly efforts on the part of insurance companies in trying to discriminate between those of their clients who are careful and those who are careless.

In practice, the tort system in many areas operates alongside other devices. In the field of industrial safety, for example, employers have to meet safety standards imposed by government agencies in addition to being liable for compensating injured workmen. The effect of imposing minimum safety standards may be to deny workers and employers the opportunity of bargaining over conditions below the minimum level, and this may be a serious criticism from an allocative standpoint. Such regulation may however have corresponding advantages particularly if we wish to allow society to express paternalistic urges. Much industrial legislation has been aimed at preventing practices that were thrown up by bargaining in labour markets, and the greater part of such legislation can only be rationalised by appeal to essentially non-economic arguments such as a desire to ensure that workers enjoy relatively safe working conditions, even if privately the workers would not be prepared to sacrifice wages on the scale required to finance the improvements. Economists in favour of free bargaining, spontaneous market outcomes and the tort system are generally rather dismissive of such paternalism but there can be little doubt of the political power of such arguments. If there is one lesson that economics can offer in the context of tort, it is that discussion which fails to take full account of both the allocative and the distributive effects of law and other institutions is ill-informed and may well be misleading as a guide both to what is happening at present and equally to what might happen if the structure of the law were to be modified.

FURTHER READING

A great deal has been written on tort in recent times both by economists and others. Amongst the main proponents of the tort system is Posner, whose text on law and economics (Posner 1977) is a good place to start. An alternative introduction to the economics of tort is Hirsch (1979). Discussion of economic aspects of liability assignment has flourished: see Brown (1973) Diamond (1974) and Diamond and Mirrlees (1975). For an introduction to the more critical approach of some economists to tort see the Introduction to Burrows and Veljanovski (1981). The difficulties of private insurance markets are discussed in Ehrlich and Becker (1972) and Rothschild and Stiglitz (1976).

There are many applications of the main arguments. Probably the best-known economics-based work on accidents is Calabresi (1970). For a critical treatment see Atiyah (1980). For a description of the New Zealand no-fault scheme see Harris (1974), whilst for a description of the English system see Royal Commission (1978) or Elliot and Street (1968). Industrial safety is discussed by Phillips (1976) and Smith (1979). On pollution see Burrows (1979) and Ogus and Richardson (1977).

Amongst the many applications not discussed in the chapter are the questions of legal and medical malpractice. On this see Calabresi (1977), Hirsch (1979) and Veljanovski and Whelan (1980). A second area is that of misrepresentation, on which see Bishop (1980).

8

Contract

CONTRACTS AND THE COST OF CONTRACTING

The processes of exchange and trade are fundamental to all economies. In market economies, goods and services are generally but not invariably exchanged for money since money represents generalised purchasing power. Money is a device that enables traders to economise on the number of transactions through which they have to proceed in moving from their initial endowment of goods and services to some preferred final position. The farmer sells corn in return for money which he can then spend directly on food, clothes, tractors or whatever. Without the convenience of money he would have to arrange an elaborate sequence of barter transactions (or swaps) in the course of which he may find himself buying and selling goods with which he has no direct concern. The costs of touting round amongst other buyers and sellers in this way will generally be much higher than those of dealing in currency.

Contracts, rather like money, are also devices for facilitating trade and economising on the costs of making transactions. By trading in promises for future delivery traders can reduce uncertainty about the future: they can assure themselves of supplies and and can fix some prices in advance that they would otherwise only be able to predict rather vaguely. Although the object of entering contracts is to reduce or avoid various kinds of uncertainty, contracts themselves are more liable than many other methods of trading to give rise to uncertainty. Whilst the thought of entering a contract may appeal to a seller because it enables

him to secure a price for his product in advance, and thus
enables him to avoid the chance that the market in the
product will fall, he knows perfectly well that if the market
does fall, his buyer may be tempted to cancel the contract and
to buy elsewhere at the new, lower price. A system of contract
law has not only to enable parties to exchange promises and
establish obligations, but has also to enable parties to have
confidence that adequate safeguards are provided against
breach by their contracting partners.

The provision of safeguards is important not only when the
parties are making a deal in which both sides are making
promises about delivering goods, services or money in the
future. Even where a simple transaction like walking into a
shop and buying a shirt is concerned, the parties to the
exchange may be anxious to establish various rights and
obligations in the event of certain contingencies. Some sort of
agreement is needed as to who is to be responsible if the shirt
should prove to be defective and what is to happen if the
customer's cheque is dishonoured and so forth. Thus, even
where the goods and money change hands immediately after
agreement has been reached, a framework of rules is needed
to deal with the various contingencies that may follow. In
England these rules are codified in the Sale of Goods Act
1979, although this Act includes the provision (s.62(2)) that
the rules of common law continue to apply except insofar as
they are inconsistent with the Act. The net result of this is
that consumers may enter the great variety of everyday
transactions without having to concern themselves with the
minutiae of the terms on which they are buying.

The principal object of contract law is to provide a
framework within which parties can establish and exchange
bundles of rights and obligations. It may to a greater or lesser
degree itself set down what is to happen in certain
circumstances, but must in any event offer parties the
opportunity to formulate enforceable agreements of many
kinds and enable them to seek remedies in the event of
agreements being broken. In the first instance it is worth
stressing that it is the existence of *any* set of rules governing
contracts, rather than the existence of rules with particular

characteristics, that is most useful for traders. It does not matter that the traders may choose to reject most or even all of the arbitrary rules we posit. Any rules are better than no rules, since they will provide a starting point for negotiation and save traders from having to 'start from scratch' every time and laboriously piece together the clauses of a contract. Under such circumstances many opportunities for mutually beneficial exchange will be missed, and traders will opt to settle for uncertainty about the future rather than incur the costs of setting up contracts that could reduce their uncertainty. If one views the nature of a capitalist economy as the unremitting search for more valuable ways of using existing resources, any elimination of barriers to exchange is likely to be socially valuable.

Having argued that any old set of rules, around which traders can negotiate and bargain, is likely to be preferred to a régime of no explicit rules, one or two caveats must be entered. In the first place, there are devices other than explicit rules which may impose the necessary constraints upon traders. Custom and practice, whether backed up by a formal set of written down rules or not, may be a perfectly effective framework within which to conduct trade. Traders' reputations will be very important and will be enquired into by prospective trading partners. Those who are persistently breaking promises will soon become identified and will find it increasingly difficult to trade. As Posner has argued, one can have an economic theory of contract without a formal system of contract law and without a well developed form of currency. It may look primitive and it may be rather cumbersome, but it will be performing the same function of ensuring that traders keep their promises and of assigning the risks inherent in trade between the parties (Posner, 1980). Indeed, as we will argue later in this chapter, custom and practice may perform a key role in keeping down the costs of making transactions even in a highly developed economy such as our own where a wide array of explicit legal machinery is very often available but not used.

The second reason why one set of rules may be superior to another is that although both sets may enable traders to reduce their transaction costs as compared with those that would be incurred in the absence of any rules at all, one set of rules may reduce these transaction costs by a greater amount than the other. There are some sorts of rules which are likely to be closer to the requirements of traders than others, and it seems quite clear that the closer are the 'official suggestions' to the terms to which the parties would gravitate *if it were costless to negotiate terms*, then the lower will be the costs of reaching agreement. To express the matter differently, the costs associated with making a transaction comprise both the costs of negotiating terms and the costs associated with any remaining imperfections, and parties will always be anxious to minimise the costs of negotiation, given the quality of the contractual terms. An empirical example of this argument is discussed in the following chapter. It concerns the way in which traders make allowance (if any) in international contracts for the increasing volatility of foreign exchange rates. Traders can bargain around any rule, but the recent changes that have taken place in the English law on the subject of foreign money obligations have affected the costs to traders of reaching what they regard as desirable terms. The change in the presumption made by the courts means that if parties want the old rules to apply they may have to make specific reference to the fact in their negotiations. If large numbers of contracts should be found to involve explicit agreements to use the old rules rather than the new ones then one might doubt the wisdom of the legal reforms that have taken place. Equally however, if many parties are able to abandon their previous practice of including clauses which set aside the old rules, then the reforms might be welcomed on the grounds that they have evidently reduced the costs associated with establishing terms that suit the parties.

Readers familiar with texts on contract law will already be aware that the treatment of the subject is rather different here. Our emphasis on the economic functions of contracts and contract law is designed to help provide a common conceptual base from which an understanding of contract law can spring. Amongst the advantages of our approach is that it enables one to make more sense of the way in which contract law is used in everyday life. Businessmen often make agreements that are not strictly enforceable legally because they try to short-cut the 'offer-acceptance' sequence: they often make agreements that are incomplete and sometimes difficult to interpret: they very often fail to pursue a legal remedy when there is one available. Legal practice has been able to come to terms with these difficulties: rulings have been made about criteria for enforceability and for interpretation. If we consider for example the 'offer-acceptance' sequence, it is very often observed that a buyer will respond to an offer on the standard terms of a prospective seller by despatching an order on his own standard terms, even though these may be quite different from the terms of offer. In such instances, under English law, it has been established that: '. . . in most cases when there is a "battle of forms" there is a contract as soon as the last of the forms is sent and received without objection being taken to it' (per Lord Denning in *Butler Machine Tool Co. v. Ex.-Cell-O Corp.* [1977]: see Major, 1980). This ruling enables the lacuna created by the existence of high bargaining costs to be filled.

BASIC ELEMENTS

The starting point for our own analysis is a somewhat abstract one. The object of a contract is taken to be to establish the assignment of gains and losses associated with the various contingencies that may befall agreements about the exchange of goods and services. If taken literally, this would entail the contracting parties making an exhaustive list of all the possible outcomes that might result from their agreeing to trade and agreeing what is to happen in each instance. In practice, such procedures would be desperately time-consuming and costly. A great number of ways have been found of reducing the resource costs of forming contracts. Parties can rely upon trade practice and custom to determine the assignment of gains and losses that may commonly result in their particular line of business, or parties can rely upon the courts applying well-known principles in seeking to infer from contracts what the parties intended to happen under certain contingencies that are not explicitly covered by the contract itself. Further, the use of standard form contracts enables parties to economise on (by sharing) the costs of devising relatively thorough contracts which are robust enough to serve many trading purposes rather than being custom-designed for a single deal.

A second line of argument says that there may be pressures other than those exerted by implicit or explicit contractual terms, which militate in favour of parties finding cheap solutions in the event of problems over a contract. This argument relies upon the observation that a great number of contracts are not isolated instances of parties wanting to trade with one another but rather will be occurring in the context of a continuing trading relationship (see for example, Macaulay, 1963 or Beale and Dugdale, 1975). The result of this is likely to be that parties will have powerful incentives to agree upon how to resolve a conflict without pursuing legal remedies that may, strictly speaking, be available under the contract. This argument is in no way inconsistent with our starting point. To the extent that it is mostly concerned with whether parties will take action when a contract has failed, it is only a rather indirect matter at this preliminary stage, and one that we do not pursue.

Returning to the question of what a contract really is, we have established thus far that it will entail a more or less thorough list of provisions about how certain contingencies are to be handled. In the course of contractual negotiations either party is free to withdraw. This is likely to happen if either one of the parties comes to the conclusion that he could get more attractive terms from another trader or if either party comes to the conclusion that the prospect offered by going ahead with the contract is simply not attractive. It may very often be quite difficult for the trader to assess the attractiveness of a contract: even experienced traders may find it quite difficult to assess the probabilities with which various contingencies will occur and thus find it difficult to measure the expected costs and benefits of going ahead with a deal. Nevertheless one can fairly confidently assert that parties acting voluntarily will sign contracts only when they think that the expected revenues or benefits of so doing exceed the expected costs. Note that costs may refer not simply to outgoings but to other opportunities. If A contracts to deliver 100 widgets to B this will mean that he is excluding the possibility of selling the widgets to C. Equally, agreeing to supply widgets precludes him from using his factory for the manufacture of other sorts of items. Thus, contracts may be unexpectedly costly to perform if it should emerge after the agreement has been made that the resources could have been exploited in some other more profitable way. That the firm will still make a profit of £50 may be relatively small consolation if it should turn out subsequently that an opportunity of making a profit of £500 is thereby foregone.

It is possible at this stage to argue that the trader, when he makes a contract, has a view about the possible outcomes that may be encapsulated in the form of a probability distribution relating the likelihood of making different amounts of net profit or loss. To think about the matter in this way has the merit that it enables one to assign a single value to the prospect represented by the contract. By discounting future costs and receipts at a rate appropriate to the trader and by assigning the relevant probability to the net present value of each possible outcome, one can reach a figure that represents the expected net present value of the contract to the trader. Applying the usual analysis of behaviour under uncertainty one can then make an adjustment that allows for the trader's attitude to risk. If after all this the two prospective contractors both find their discounted profit levels to be positive then a deal will be struck.

Some important implications emerge from characterising the problem in this rather formal way. If the parties have different attitudes towards risk for example then it will be possible to change the net profits being enjoyed by the parties by certain sorts of changes in the contractual terms. Making provision for the party that is less risk averse to assume risks that would otherwise fall on the other party is one such method. The drawbacks of using this approach for present purposes are however rather major ones. Although much of the work being done by contemporary economists in the area of contract exploits precisely this sort of methodology (see for example Diamond and Maskin, 1979 and Shavell, 1980), it would hamper our efforts to illustrate that economics can be used to make observations about contract law that are intelligible to non-specialist economists.

CONTRACT, PRICE AND THE ASSIGNMENT OF RISKS

The profit-maximising firm or trader can be viewed as scanning the available trading opportunities and opting for the one which offers the prospect of greatest net benefit. These net benefits will be conditioned not only by the price offered under the contract but also by the contractual terms themselves. Although competitive forces and evolutionary pressures may encourage traders in a market to rely for the most part upon similar contracts, there may be circumstances in which a buyer or seller may find himself able to clinch a deal by varying contractual provisions rather than price.

The notion of varying contractual terms may be a straightforward matter of inserting an extra clause in an effort to make a sale. It may also however be more broadly interpreted. A good example arises in the context of international trade. An English trader contemplating doing business with a Swiss trader has the choice between offering to make the contract subject to English law or Swiss law. His choice in the matter will influence the pattern of rights and obligations created, and the trader will have to take a view about which pattern of rules he prefers, and the price at which he will agree to trade in each case. It may be for instance that the English trader would feel that he was better protected from exchange risk under English law. By calculating the probability that these exchange risks might be relevant and the degree to which the net present value of his proceeding with the transaction might be affected, the English trader will be able to infer the price to be stipulated in the contract. This price will be higher the lower is the protection afforded to the trader under different contingencies and the more likely he thinks it that such contingencies will arise. Thus he might be prepared to trade at SF180 under English law but only at SF200 under Swiss law.

It is generally true that there is no reason in principle why most risks under a contract should be assigned one way rather than another. If a seller is prevented from meeting his commitments because his goods are destroyed by flood or fire, there is no obvious reason why he, rather than the buyer, should be responsible for the damages that non-delivery inflicts upon the buyer. Arrangement for some third party to provide the goods could be made at the expense of either the buyer or the seller. In instances where there is a reasonably high chance for example that goods will be damaged in transit, the risk of loss may be assumed by either the seller or the buyer. Under c.i.f. contracts buyers pay for the insurance of the goods in transit whilst under f.o.b. contracts the insurance of cargoes is a matter for negotiation (see for example, Rose 1979). The price agreed under the contract will clearly be influenced by the arrangements over insurance that the parties make.

RISK AND THE CHEAPEST INSURER

As has already been implied to argue that all risks may *in principle* be assigned either way is not to argue that all risks will be unambiguously assigned, nor is it to argue that the parties will be indifferent to the assignment, nor yet is it to argue that the price change associated with a change in assignment will exactly reflect the cost of absorbing the risk. Generally speaking, one party will be relatively better equipped to deal with some sorts of risk. This superiority is something that the party is most likely to exploit in bargaining. It may result either because the parties have different attitudes towards risk, or because the assignment of liability may itself influence the behaviour of the parties and thus the probability that the risk will materialise.

The way in which one party may exploit another party's

risk aversion, or any differences between the attitudes towards risk of the two parties, is explored further in chapter 11 in the context of negotiations over out-of-court settlements. As far as pre-contractual negotiations are concerned, the possibilities of exploiting such differences are limited by a party's capacity to break off or threaten to break off negotiations and search for a new contracting partner. Nevertheless it may be that buyers and sellers in particular sorts of markets have (systematically) different attitudes towards risk, or by specialising in trading in certain sorts of risk are able to bear them more comfortably. In such instances risks will regularly be assumed by one or other 'side' of the market. A good example is the sort of contract into which authors generally enter with publishers. In return for an advance, and an agreement that the publisher will meet the costs of production, the author agrees to take, let us say, 10 per cent of any revenue from sales of the book. This entails publishers taking fairly major risks as compared with authors since many of the publisher's costs will be incurred before it is known whether the book will sell or not. There are of course exceptions. It is said that Keynes came in the 1930s to an agreement with his publishers (Macmillan) under which he absorbed the bulk of the risk attending the success of his books. In his biography Harrod (1951) recounts that Keynes agreed to meet all the production costs and put his publisher on 10 per cent of the gross. Most authors however deny themselves such a gamble: they are prepared to pay a substantial premium in return for a less variable income from the work.

The other factor which may influence the assignment of risk is the so-called 'moral hazard' problem. If parties are able to shift liability for certain risks to others, they may behave more carelessly in various important respects than they would do otherwise. In many instances a party may not directly absorb a risk itself, but take out an insurance policy to cover it. This does not however make any real difference since the premium charged by the insurance company will reflect the view they take of the risk, and the premium will be reflected in the price which the party taking out the insurance is prepared to pay (or receive) under the contract.

If the risks are largely 'objective' and independent of human action they may well be straightforward to insure, but equally the parties themselves should be able to reach agreement on the price that they put upon such risks. It is however very often the case that risks are not entirely independent of human action or inaction. The risk of fire for example may depend quite heavily on the extent to which a trader is careful to take preventive action, even though fires may often seem to be 'accidents'.

What is important however is that some parties may be able to prevent accidents more cheaply than others. A storm at sea for example may cause damage to a cargo if it has not been very securely packed and loaded. The incentives that those responsible for packing and loading have to exercise care may be influenced by the assignment of risk as between buyer, seller and shipper. If the cargo consists of glassware for example it will be important that the initial packing is done very carefully, since it will generally be much cheaper to take precautions at that stage than subsequently. This kind of result will probably require that the seller of the goods rather than the buyer assume responsibility for the safe carriage of the cargo. Any other arrangement might well entail the shipper having to repack the load or a much higher insurance premium being asked and so on.

It is interesting to note that in the longer term, if it becomes widely realised that the safety of cargoes depends upon several 'links in the chain' between seller and buyer there may be quite strong pressures for the relevant operations to be amalgamated under unified control. If a single agency becomes responsible for both packing and loading, the two activities may be better co-ordinated from a safety viewpoint, and the improvements to the accident record which results should enable such agencies to make more competitive quotes than non-integrated firms. This is an example of how cost-reducing pressures may drive firms to organise themselves more efficiently and may eliminate the need to rely on contracts between firms. Indeed there are some authors (see for example Coase, 1937 or Williamson 1979) who argue that the very existence of firms is a reflection of the high costs of making contracts and transactions. Thus, establishing a firm is a device, like money, that enables entrepreneurs to economise on transactions costs. It could be argued that one of the factors encouraging the growth of firms is thus a concern to reap further economies and to minimise the need to rely upon contracting partners.

NON-PERFORMANCE

We have argued thus far that contracts are concerned with the assignment of risks between the parties and that the contract price will reflect this assignment, whether implicitly or explicitly. One class of risk that deserves closer attention is the risk that one or other or both parties may wish to withdraw from a contract that they have entered. We look now at the terms that might be expected to govern such withdrawals.

The conditions under which firms are allowed to escape from contractual obligations may themselves be written into the contract or be a matter that can be readily resolved. If firm A has agreed to supply 100 widgets to B for £50, but finds that he could instead sell the goods to a foreign buyer for £100, then he may withdraw his promise to supply B, but at the same time compensate B for any higher price that B has to pay to obtain the widgets from some other supplier. This does of course make economic sense. If B can buy from C at £70 then it is desirable that A should sell to the foreigner and compensate B accordingly, for that way B remains as well off as he would have been had the contract been performed whilst A makes an additional net profit of £30 compared with the profit expected under the contract with B. No one loses and the resources find their ways into more highly-valued uses than would have been the case had performance of the contract been insisted upon. The duty of B to mitigate damages and to buy from the next cheapest available supplier of comparable widgets is also soundly based on the same economic principle of maximising net advantage to the parties without either party being disappointed and doing worse than expected under the contract. Equally straightforward is the case where both parties find it expedient to cancel the contract. There is clearly no advantage to be gained from insisting that the contract must be honoured when both parties have decided that they would themselves prefer to withdraw. This situation is clearly one where bilateral discharge is the efficient solution.

There may be other instances where the parties to a contract recognise that there are some fairly common barriers to performance for which they wish to take explicit account. One such barrier is the likelihood that a ship carrying a cargo is held up outside a harbour and is thus delayed in delivering its goods. In such circumstances the owner of the ship incurs a loss because he is prevented from renting the ship to a third party during the course of the delay. It is common for such delay to be specifically catered for in charterparties by means of a liquidated damages clause. Under such clauses, the amount of damages to be paid per day in the event of delay is specified in the contract, being referred to as 'demurrage'. Similar sorts of provision are often made in construction contracts, where delay may be very costly for owners and/or for other contractors involved in the project.

One interesting legal provision in this context that is much more difficult to rationalise is the prohibition of so-called 'penalty' clauses. Under this provision, amounts specified under the liquidated damages head must not exceed the actual losses involved. Should they do so, the clause is unenforceable, and all the convenience of such arrangements disappears. It is to a related problem that we turn for the last part of our general discussion of contract law.

BARGAINING POWER AND UNCONSCIONABILITY

It is perhaps typical that an area about which many lawyers expect economists to have a lot to say should be one that has attracted rather less attention. It is not a little ironical to observe that this lack of interest can be quite readily attributed to the fact that the economic model assumes that contracts are entered rationally. Individuals pursuing self-interest will never enter contracts on terms that can really be said to be 'unfair'. The observation that courts are on occasion prepared to reject contracts or to alter contractual provisions on the grounds that an unconscionable bargain is involved suggests that the law regards individuals as being fallible in a way that economics does not permit.

In the explicitly individualistic and subjectivist world of traditional economic theory consumers are sovereign: they do not trade on terms that will leave them worse off, and thus there are no grounds for interfering in the contracts they make. Having said that, it is relevant to note that bargaining very often involves parties who are quite different in their market power if by market power one means the market value of a party's assets. This is a quite different matter from bargaining power in the economic sense. If we take a pair of contractors and establish the upper and lower limits on the contract price that will result in a deal being struck, bargaining power is something that might be measured by reference to the relationship between the contract price agreed and these upper and lower bounds. A person owning only a small parcel of land may hold out for a very high price from a property company that wants the land to complete the area it needs for a housing development. There will be an upper limit beyond which the property company will not bid just as there will be a lower limit below which the individual will not sell. In such circumstances the outcome is in some respects indeterminate, since there will be a wide range of prices at which both the property company and the individual could strike a mutually beneficial deal. It may of course be that some individuals would be better at guessing the upper price limit to which the property developer is prepared to go than others. The poor and ignorant may sell under such circumstances at a much lower price than someone with more experience in such matters. Although this may seem morally a rather unattractive solution, it is perhaps worth pointing out first that such transactions will not normally leave the poor and ignorant worse off than they would otherwise have been and secondly that the prospect of being able to make such profits will tend to attract new traders into such areas with the result that increased competition will eliminate the profits being made. There may nevertheless be instances in which individuals find themselves victims of some particularly harsh term or terms in a contract. Indeed one might argue that in any 'civilised' economy, society will be prepared to offer some protection to those who seem to be 'exploited', even if this is at the expense of preventing some potentially beneficial transactions from taking place.

Under the common law in England a contract can be avoided if it was made under duress. This provision offers only minimal help, but is complemented, first by various equitable rules and secondly by various statutory provisions. The most interesting (for present purposes) of the reliefs available under equity provisions is the notion of an 'unconscionable' bargain. 'The classic example of an unconscionable bargain is where advantage has been taken of a young, inexperienced or ignorant person to introduce a term which no sensible well-advised person or party would have accepted' (per Browne-Wilkinson J in *Multiservice Bookbinding Ltd. v. Marden* [1978] at 550). It is of course very difficult to decide whether any particular bargain is unconscionable, although it is probably fair to say that the terms of a contract must be rather harsh before the criterion is met.

The Unfair Contract Terms Act 1977 is perhaps more generous, since it substitutes a test of unreasonableness for the more stringent test of unconscionability. Schedule 2 of the Act sets down 'guidelines' for the application of the reasonableness test that include:

(a) the strength of the bargaining positions of the parties relative to each other, taking into account (among other things) alternative means by which the customer's requirements could have been met.

Provisions of this kind may afford considerable help, after the event, to those who have suffered under a contract, but they do not come 'free'. If sellers find themselves becoming more vulnerable to such actions, they will modify their behaviour. They may try harder to spot bad risks and refuse to trade with certain groups of buyers, but more likely, they will raise the price at which they offer goods and services sufficiently to cover the additional costs of defending possible legal actions.

An area to which special rules have often, but not always, applied is that of moneylending. Until the Usury Laws Repeal Act 1854, there had been major restrictions on the terms which lenders could fix. Between 1854 and 1900 when the Moneylenders Act was passed the terms upon which money could be lent were subject only to the equitable rule of unconscionability. The Moneylenders Acts of 1900 and 1927 have subsequently been overtaken by the Consumer Credit Act 1974. Under this new statute, criteria are set down in section 138 (i) which govern whether a set of terms in a mortgage may be viewed as 'extortionate'. Some doubt seems to persist about the relation between the criteria in the 1974 Act and those in the earlier statutes of 1900 and 1927 (see Wilkinson, 1980, and Bowles, 1981), although the general opinion seems to be that when the courts are deciding whether the rate of interest being paid by a debtor is exorbitant they will use as guidelines the principles established under the earlier moneylending legislation.

Limitations of space preclude any further discussion of the interesting series of cases in which arguments over the successive sets of criteria are documented. What can be said in conclusion is that changes in public attitudes towards the victims of hard bargains are expressed through changes in statute. In striking a balance between allowing as much scope as possible to parties to make mutually beneficial trades and protecting the weak from oppression, Parliament has to weigh a variety of conflicting interests. If economists err on the side of promoting trade it may be because they know more about trade than about oppression.

CONCLUDING REMARKS

The existence of contract law may be seen as a response to the high costs of making transactions. Contract law enables such costs to be reduced provided that it establishes clearly and precisely how the court will respond in those instances where a contract has failed for some reason not explicitly catered for by the parties. Whilst it is useful for contract law to contain clauses or provisions that mimic as closely as possible the pattern of risk assignment and remedies that bargaining parties would ideally like, the central requirement is that the rules to be applied in the absence of express agreement are clear. If there remains ambiguity then traders will incur higher costs in making transactions than is necessary.

The price which traders agree under a contract will generally reflect their perceptions of the gains and losses that they can expect to make, given the terms (both implied and express) of the contract. Any ambiguity in the law will thus trigger either a rise in the risk premium which traders add to the price at which they are prepared to trade, and/or a rise in the costs that the parties incur in settling between themselves how to cater for contingencies that are uncertainly treated by the law.

The main strand of criticism of this model in which traders reach a cost-minimising set of contracts and contract terms is based on the argument that contractors will rarely find it expedient to pursue a formal legal remedy. This tends to reduce still further the significance attaching to the legal rules and to give greater importance to the customary ways of resolving disputes and assigning risks within particular markets and within the continuing relationship between particular traders.

As in so many areas where economics is applied to real world problems the apparent conflict between different theories may seem to limit the value of economists. Such a view may be mistaken to the extent that the theories actually conflict rather less than it may seem at first glance. Our emphasis in this chapter on the 'neo-classical' theory at the expense of the 'trading relationship' approach reflects a concern to examine the question of contract law from a general point of view. Efforts to understand why contracts in particular markets tend to take a typical and distinctive form may, on the other hand, benefit from the greater scope that the trading relationship approach accords to market detail.

Having in this chapter looked at some of the fundamentals of contract law, we move in the next to consider how some of these arguments may be applied in the search for an understanding of how contract, and to a lesser degree other areas of law, operate in an international context.

FURTHER READING

Contract law can be approached in several ways. For a traditional treatment the reader is referred to a standard text such as *Cheshire and Fifoot's Law of Contract* (Furmston, 1981). In the traditional economics-based approach the law of contract is viewed as a device for facilitating the exchange of promises and for assigning risks between the parties. Clear statements of this position are to be found in Posner (1977) and Kronman and Posner (1979).

Economists and lawyers are however turning increasingly to the view that contracts are best understood by putting emphasis on the role of transactions costs and on the continuing relationship between traders. Two good, and readily-available, sources for this new view are Macneil (1981) and Williamson (1981), both of which draw heavily upon well-known earlier writings by these two authors such as Macneil (1974, 1978) and Williamson (1975, 1979). This 'new approach', outlined also in Beale (1980), draws in part upon earlier empirical studies by Macaulay (1963) and Beale and Dugdale (1975).

For further discussion of the development of the law, see Atiyah (1979, 1981) whilst for some other applications of economics to contract law see Harris, Ogus and Phillips (1979) or Kronman (1978).

9

Foreign Money Obligations

In the previous two chapters we have looked at some of the general economic arguments that may be germane to discussion of contract and tort law. This chapter explores some of the additional problems which emerge when it comes to applying some of these general arguments in the context of foreign money obligations. We concentrate for the most part upon the law of contract as it applies in international transactions but make passing mention of tort cases involving parties from different countries. The principal issue upon which we focus is the choice of the currency in which awards of damages (or judgment debts or whatever) are to be denominated and the allied question of the choice of interest rates at which any compensation for delay is to be awarded. To the extent that English law on these matters has undergone drastic reform in the course of the last decade we will be concerned to make some comments on the processes by which law comes to be reformed as well as on the reforms themselves. We begin by outlining the law as it stood before the landmark case of *Miliangos v Frank* [1975] and then proceed to the questions of why reform was instituted and of whether the reforms have satisfactorily resolved the issues which prompted them.

ENGLISH LAW PRE-1975

English law before 1975 recognised sterling as the only currency in which actions could be brought or awards made.

The accompanying requirement was that if damage had been sustained or felt in a foreign currency, the amount of damage was to be calculated as a sterling sum reached by applying the exchange rate prevailing on the date when the damage was incurred (or the contract was breached) to the sum of foreign currency involved. This was referred to as the 'breach date rule' or the 'sterling rule'. The plaintiff would be compensated for any delay by an award of interest calculated by applying simple (but not compound) English interest rates over the period between the breach or tort taking place and the date when judgment on the case was finally given. This rule applied not only to cases where one or other party was English (and the case was brought in England) but also to cases where neither party was English but the matter was brought under English law.

Straightforward as this rule was, the ever-increasing volatility of exchange rates during the early 1970s came to mean that some traders were losing heavily under the 'sterling rule'. In particular, a plaintiff trading in a currency that was strengthening against sterling following a breach of contract would lose out, and the longer the delay between breach and resolution of the case the greater would these losses be. If for example the breach entailed a loss of $200 to an American trader at a time when the pound stood at $2 = £1, and the exchange rate moved to $1.8 = £1 before the matter was resolved, the American would be awarded £100. This sum was the equivalent of $200 at the date of breach even though it will now buy the American only $180. Thus, even though English interest rates would have been awarded on the £100 to compensate for the delay, the American might well think himself to have been harshly treated.

From the American's point of view there are two quite distinct things to worry about. In the first place the inevitable delay between breach and judgment might give rise to considerable losses as a result of currency fluctuations and thus leave him worse off than he was when he entered the contract initially. Secondly, his contracting partner will be given an incentive to further delay settlement of the case. As long as sterling is weakening, the defendant gains from using delaying tactics provided only that he is not doing so too blatantly. Only rarely do the courts (explicitly) penalise parties for using deliberate measures to cause delay and, particularly if it seems likely that the matter will be settled out of court, such penalties may not be taken very seriously.

In economic terms it is the second of these two problems which is the more serious. Following the argument of the previous chapter we may argue that the risk of losses from exchange rate changes is a matter that the parties can anticipate. Thus whilst in some particular instance one might sympathise with a plaintiff who has incurred currency losses, it is to be expected that parties are aware of such risks when they engage in international trade. The prospect of losses (to one or other side of a bargain) will generally be a matter that is reasonably foreseeable, with the consequence that the parties will be expected to take appropriate precautions. Further, it is to be expected that the price established under preliminary negotiation will reflect the assignment of exchange risks for which the parties either implicitly or explicitly opt. Such negotiation may entail efforts either to have the contract price expressed in one currency rather than another or to have the contract price adjusted upwards or downwards in anticipation of exchange rate movements. We look now in more detail at the relation between contract price and exchange risk and then at the problem of the incentive to delay.

(i) CONTRACT PRICE AND EXCHANGE RISK

At the time when the contract was agreed between the parties the exchange rate (to pursue the example of the previous section) may have been $2.20 = £1. Both parties realised that sterling was likely to weaken subsequently and the contract price could be taken to encapsulate the views of the parties about such risks. Thus when the American signed the contract and agreed a price of £100 to be payable in six months he guessed that by that time the £100 would correspond to only $200 rather than the $220 it represented at the exchange rate prevailing when he made the deal. If he could guess that much (and international traders cannot avoid making such judgments) then could he not equally well guess that in the event of the Englishman failing to pay up on time further delay (and thus a greater loss of dollars) would be involved? Should the answer to this be affirmative it is but a short step to argue that the American could have assigned, let us say, a 10 per cent chance to the Englishman failing to pay before sterling had weakened yet further to $1.80 = £1. The net result is that one can argue that the American interpreted the deal to receive £100 as having an expected value V of:

$$V = \quad 200 \cdot 0.9 \quad + \quad 180 \cdot 0.1 \quad = \$198$$

| = | number of dollars . received if payment is made promptly | probability + of prompt payment | no. of dollars recovered by legal action | probability legal action necessary |

Had the American been more pessimistic about the likelihood of the Englishman paying promptly or about the rate at which the dollar would strengthen he would presumably have bargained for some amount in excess of £100. To put the point slightly differently we might argue that the price included an implicit risk premium to take account of the likely losses from exchange rate fluctuations.

(ii) THE INCENTIVE TO DELAY

A pervasive problem that the American is likely to encounter when trying to calculate the value of the contract is the incentive that the sterling rule creates for miscreants to delay. If the Englishman fails to pay as agreed, the American will have to take action against him in the sure knowledge that a weakening pound puts him at a major disadvantage. Given the way we have set the example up, it *seems* that the English party does not really stand to gain (unless the interest rate applied by the court to compensate for delay lies far below the interest rate at which the Englishman can lend and borrow) from delaying. But this observation only applies to those instances where the case will be heard in court. Unless there are legal novelties or other unusual features of the case, such conflicts will generally be resolved out of court. In the latter circumstances, delay or the threat of delay has to be taken seriously by the plaintiff.

The threat to delay may be of benefit to the defendant because it will encourage the American to settle for a lower sum. The American is anxious to settle before a further weakening of sterling reduces the value of his claim, and thus will be prepared to make concessions in the search for speedy settlement. The details of these arguments about the way in which defendants can exploit the plaintiff's attitude towards risk or his concern for a rapid solution are elaborated in chapter 11 below in which we discuss the economics of litigation. For the present it is sufficient to observe that the application of the sterling rule may create incentives for one or other party in a case to delay and this may well be wasteful since legal and other resources may be used to no real benefit and also because it may discourage parties from engaging in trade that would be mutually beneficial under some different set of rules. The open-endedness of the possible losses to plaintiffs from delay by defendants, even though they may in principle be predicted, may be a major hazard for traders to overcome.

Having argued that there is at least one quite strong reason why parties might find the sterling rule rather unattractive when they are choosing the legal jurisdiction to which a contract is to be subject or are trying to negotiate a contract price which adequately reflects the risks that the parties perceive to be associated with the contract, there may be other reasons which militate in favour of its retention. The sterling rule has attractions of certainty and simplicity so that part'es can readily apprehend the consequences of proceeding under such terms. Equally, if many traders dislike such a rule they are free to bargain around it. The problem with which we are concerned here applies only when the parties have made no provisions in the contract which either implicitly or explicitly indicate the currency in which payments are to be made.

The other point which should be made is that the rule under which sums in foreign currency are translated into sterling at the date of breach, or the date when the tort occurred, only creates difficulty if exchange rates change between that date and the date when judgment is given or the matter is resolved. If currency values remain stable in relation to one another over this period then no problems arise. Note however that even under a régime of fixed exchange rates of the kind used in England prior to 1972 the occasional 'overnight' devaluation may be even more damaging to the parties as and when it occurs. Under the floating exchange rate system now used by many countries, currency fluctuations have become a widely-recognised difficulty. It was indeed a recognition of the increased volatility of exchange rates which was one of the major stimuli to the reform of English law in this area in the early part of the 1970s.

Before moving to consider the legal changes it is well to observe that the courts were conscious of the advantages of certainty that were associated with refusing to entertain claims made in any currency other than sterling. In an earlier case *Treseder-Griffin v Co-operative Insurance Society Ltd* [1956], albeit in a rather different context, Lord Denning had remarked:

. . . in England we have always looked upon a pound as a pound, whatever its international value. We have dealt in pounds for more than a thousand years − long before there were gold coins or paper notes. In all our dealings we have disregarded alike the debasement of the currency by kings and rulers or the depreciation of it by the march of time or events . . . Creditors and debtors have arranged for payment in our sterling currency in the sure knowledge that the sum they fix will be upheld by the law. A man who stipulates for a pound must take a pound when payment is made, whatever the pound is worth at that time. Sterling is the constant unit of value by which in the eye of the law everything else is measured. Prices of commodities may go up or down, other currencies may go up and down, but sterling remains the same.

Despite the convenience for the courts of having to deal only with sterling and despite the suggestion that contracting parties could anticipate currency risks by adjusting contract price, increasing pressure led to the decision by the courts to abandon the traditional sterling rule. This decision is described in *Cheshire and North's Private International Law* (North, 1979) as being one of 'major commercial and financial significance'.

THE MILIANGOS DECISION

Although the House of Lords' decision in *Miliangos v Frank* [1975] is the most widely referred to, the first case in which judgment was given in a foreign currency involved an award by an arbitrator, *Jugoslavenska Oceanska Plovidba v Castle Investment Co. Inc.* [1974]. The same policy was followed by the Court of Appeal in *Schorsch Meier G.m.b.H. v Henin* [1975] and shortly after that by the House of Lords in *Miliangos*.

The facts of the *Miliangos* case are quite straightforward and bear a reasonably close resemblance to those of the hypothetical case discussed earlier in this chapter. An English company, George Frank Ltd, had agreed to buy some polyester yarn from a Swiss national, Michael Miliangos, at a price fixed in Swiss Francs. The goods were delivered as agreed but no payments were made. At that time sterling was deteriorating rapidly in value relative to strong currencies such as the Swiss Franc. Had the court applied the sterling rule, Miliangos would have received many fewer Swiss Francs than he had originally bargained for, at least in part because of the fall in the value of sterling between the date when payment should have been made under the contract and the date when the court gave its judgment. Miliangos was allowed his claim in Swiss Francs, and the case heralded a succession of further cases in which some of the implications of this revolutionary change were tested out.

The Miliangos case posed several questions. In the first place, having decided that Miliangos be allowed his claim in Swiss Francs, the House of Lords had to give some indication of the range of circumstances in which plaintiffs would henceforth be able to pursue claims in a foreign currency. They were cautious and limited application of the new

principle to cases of the same kind as Miliangos. Their
Lordships confined their approval of a change in the breach-
date rule to foreign money obligations arising under contracts
whose proper law was that of a foreign country. It was not
long however before the change was extended to other areas.
In *Services Europe Atlantique Sud v Stockholms
Rederiaktiebolag S.V.E.A.* [1978] it was established that the
court can give judgment for a sum in foreign currency as
damages for breach of contract, and the new rule was further
extended to cover actions for damages in tort in *The Despina
R* [1978]. The requirement that the proper law of the
contract be the law of a foreign country has also been relaxed
(North, 1979, pp 714 – 8).

In addition to the question of the scope that the new rule
should have, the Miliangos case raised the problem of how
interest payments in such cases were to be calculated. In
awarding damages to compensate plaintiffs for delay, the
courts have discretion under the Law Reform (Miscellaneous
Provisions) Act 1934 to award interest at simple but not
compound interest rates. The House of Lords referred the
case back to the trial judge for determination of appropriate
interest payments. In *Miliangos v George Frank Ltd. (No. 2)*
[1976], Bristow J. held that Swiss, rather than English,
interest rates were the correct measure of the losses resulting
from the delay that Miliangos had suffered. Further
discussion of the choice of interest rate is deferred until the
next section.

A third question which the Miliangos case posed was
whether the court would have dealt with Miliangos in the
same way if sterling had been strengthening against the Swiss
Franc, rather than losing ground. Dr Mann in his classic
work *The Legal Aspect of Money* (Mann, 1971) suggests that
the old sterling rule might have looked rather different had it
been developed in times when sterling was a weak
international currency rather than a strong one. Until sterling
became a weakening currency there was no incentive for
plaintiffs to seek to avoid awards in sterling. When the House
of Lords reviewed the sterling rule in the *Havana Railways*
[1961] case, Lord Denning had expressed the matter plainly.

Having stated that the sterling rule had been instituted at a time when sterling was stable, he argued that the rule should be retained even though sterling had become less stable: if a foreign creditor 'chooses to sue in our courts rather than his own, he must put up with the consequences'. In the *Miliangos* case the tone of the argument was quite different and the foreign creditor was now to be the party to whom protection was afforded: 'the creditor has no concern with pounds sterling: for him what matters is that a Swiss Franc for good or ill should remain a Swiss Franc'.

The matter at issue is the degree to which the plaintiff should be offered a choice over the rules which he invites the court to apply. What, for example, should happen to the foreign creditor whose currency is weakening against sterling? Subsequent cases suggest that the answer to this question is that the award should in any event be made in the relevant foreign currency, even if this should bestow an advantage on the defendant. It should of course be remembered that the court only has to make a choice of currency in the event that there is no express or implied term in the contract which determines the currency in which payments are to be made. Otherwise it seems clear that it is the plaintiff's currency which is to be decisive, subject only to Lord Wilberforce's comments in *The Despina R* [1979], a case in which the House of Lords extended the Miliangos principle of making awards in a foreign currency to instances of tort. Lord Wilberforce comments:

I wish to make clear that I would not approve of a hard and fast rule that in all cases where a plaintiff suffers a loss or damage in a foreign currency the right currency to take for the purpose of his claim is 'the plaintiff's currency'. I should . . emphasize that it does not suggest the use of a personal currency attached, like nationality, to a plaintiff, but a currency which he is able to show is that in which he normally conducts trading operations.

That is to say that if a case arises in which a Swiss party, or a party normally trading in Swiss Francs, is seeking to recover payment from an English party and there is no clear indication from the contract what the parties intended, then the Swiss Franc is the currency in which an award will be made irrespective of whether the Franc is gaining or losing ground *vis-à-vis* sterling on the foreign exchanges. The *Despina* case must be treated with some caution however because the decision there concerns only the tort of negligence and damage to property. In addition, the words of Lord Wilberforce quoted in the previous paragraph contain the caveat that there may be circumstances in which the plaintiff's use of his own currency is too remote a consequence of the injured party's behaviour for the tortfeasor to be expected to compensate him for any resulting losses.

A different way of expressing the thrust of the new rules is to argue that the change in rules has had the effect of shifting liability for exchange risks from creditors (or those suffering from the commission of torts) to debtors (or tortfeasors). Under the pre-1975 rules, people in the position of Miliangos (that is creditors) were losing when sterling was weakening and gaining when it was strengthening, because their award would be based on the sterling equivalent at the date of breach. People in the position of Frank (that is debtors) were not absorbing any risk either way: their liability to pay damages was unaffected by changes in exchange rates. Under the new rules, the creditor is now put in the 'neutral' position of being unaffected by currency value fluctuations, whilst the debtor stands to gain or lose depending upon the direction in which exchange rates are moving.

The inference to which one is driven by thinking about the new rules in this kind of way is that although they may look different from the traditional rule, they seem in most respects to have similar advantages and disadvantages. In the first place, cases only have to be brought if the intentions of the parties about which currency is to be used are unclear. It seems most likely that the presumption that parties are willing and able to think about and negotiate over contingencies like exchange rate fluctuations may be mistaken. In economising on the costs of transacting, parties may fail to take account of currency risks, but it cannot be argued at the same time that they are making allowance for such risks in the price that they negotiate. In the second place, the new rules do not eliminate the problem of the existence of incentives to delay. All that has happened is that the incentives now fall to different parties under different circumstances. Having said that, however, one might observe that the new rule seems 'fairer' to the extent that the party incurring a loss is being more exactly returned to the position that they would have occupied had the tort or the breach of contract not taken place. This may not be any more efficient economically, if only because of the ambiguity of the notion of the position that the person expects to reach as a result of entering the contract. For the principle of *restitutio in integrum* to work properly in the legal argument on this point, it is necessary to take it for granted that both parties enter the contract in good faith and that the contract price is independent of worries about whether the contract will be successfully discharged or about currency values.

CHOICE OF INTEREST RATE

In a recent Working Paper on Foreign Money Obligations (Law Commission, 1981) the Law Commission open one of their chapters with the observation that: 'An issue of considerable significance in the context of foreign money obligations is whether the plaintiff is entitled to interest on a debt which has not been paid on the due date or on a claim for damages' (p. 115). This section is devoted to a brief discussion, not so much of the Law Commission's assertion, but of the question of which interest rate it is appropriate to choose.

This question was considered explicitly by the trial judge in *Miliangos (No. 2)*, as indeed we mentioned in the previous section. The decision that the relevant interest rate is the one which applies in the currency in which the award is made may seem straightforward and sensible. There are however a number of technical difficulties. Principal amongst these is whether the payment of interest is to be made under the *lex fori* or the *lex causae*. We do not pursue these matters here:

the interested reader is referred to either chapter 3 of Law Commission (1981) or to North (1979). It is nevertheless possible to make some observations about the consequences that have to be confronted if, for whatever reason, a decision entails applying the interest rate which prevails upon a currency other than the one in which the award is made.

In order to illustrate our contention let us consider the determinants of interest rates and exchange rates on the world's financial markets. The volume of internationally-mobile funds is sufficiently large to ensure a close relation between (i) spot and forward exchange rates on any pair of currencies and (ii) the difference in interest rates between the two countries. The spot exchange rate is the rate at which currencies can currently be exchanged whilst the forward rate refers to the terms upon which banks and others will agree to buy or sell the currency as at some specified date in the future. The forward rate exceeds the spot rate if the balance of market opinion is that a currency will strengthen and vice versa. The relation between spot and forward rates is generally expressed as a premium or discount on the spot rate. This premium or discount will be related to interest rates because of the fact that the owners of internationally-mobile funds will compare the rate of return offered by holding the funds in safe investments in different financial centres throughout the world. An English investor with £1 million in liquid funds that he wants to invest over six months will consider, inter alia, the following strategies:

(a) buy short-term UK government securities that mature in six months;

(b) buy long-term UK government securities that mature several years hence, in the expectation of selling in six months;

(c) buy US dollars and use the proceeds to buy six month US government securities: sell the resulting dollars (a perfectly predictable number) on the forward market and thus secure a known sum of sterling in six months;

(d) as in (c), buy dollars and thence US securities but do not sell the dollars forward: trade them instead on the spot market six months hence in the hope that the exchange rate will have moved in favour of sterling by a greater amount than is suggested by rates on today's forward market.

For present purposes, it is the relation between strategies (a) and (c) that is of relevance. Both transactions involve no risk in the sense that both offer the investor a perfectly predictable sum six months hence. It takes little financial expertise to deduce that the investor will rank (a) and (c) by reference simply to the sterling sum expected under each.

Investors around the world will be doing the same sorts of calculations. Normal competitive forces will constrain all financial institutions to offer similar forward rates. The net result is that all investment funds will tend to be attracted by the same country, and that is the country where interest rates are unusually high in relation to expected movements in the currency's value. This may be somewhere with very high interest rates but with a currency upon which the forward discount is only rather small. It could equally well be somewhere with very low interest rates but a very high forward premium. Suppose for example that a return of 8 per cent is payable on a UK security, that is that £1 million spent on such securities today will yield £1.08 million in six months. Suppose further that the current spot exchange rate is $2 = £1 and that interest rates are higher in the US, standing at 12 per cent over six months. The investor's £1 million can then be used to buy $2 million worth of US securities that will be worth $2.24 million in six months. This $2.24 million can be 'sold' in advance on the forward market and will promise the investor a certain sum of sterling. If the forward discount is 10 cents so that the exchange rate is effectively $1.90, a bank will promise to buy the proceeds for £1.178947 million. This would leave the investor better off by £98,947 than if he had stayed in sterling. Had there been a premium of 10 cents on the forward market however the bank would have promised to pay only £1.06666 million for the dollars, leaving the investor worse off than he would have been had he bought UK securities. The combination of the forward discount or premium and the interest rate differential between countries will thus determine the countries to which investors are keen to switch their funds. Since governments are generally anxious to maintain investment levels, they may be forced to alter interest rates accordingly. At the same time, if many investors start to buy a country's currency on the spot market, the currency's spot price will rise and the forward premium reduced or the discount raised, given the interest rate. An initially attractive location for funds thus becomes less attractive as funds pour in there and the unusually profitable opportunity disappears.

The important lesson from all this about the legal treatment of interest rates is that currency fluctuations and interest rate differentials tend to be inversely correlated. If sterling is strengthening against the dollar, interest rates will have to be higher in the US than in England if an exodus of funds from New York is to be avoided. At the same time, if the Swiss Franc is strengthening against sterling then interest rates will be higher in England than in Switzerland.

It should be remembered that when we talk about fluctuations in exchange rates we are generally referring to changes in spot rates. Forward exchange rates are not perfect predictors of future spot rates, but are normally a good guide. If this latter were not true, one would expect speculators to find ways of exploiting the fact, and this alone would tend to improve the degree to which forward premia or discounts reflected likely movements in spot exchange rates. The conclusion that there is an inverse relation between exchange rate movements and interest rate differentials is thus preserved, although there may not be a perfect correlation between the variables.

The importance of the foregoing discussion lies in the fact that if a foreign creditor is to be protected from a weakening of sterling he should not benefit from the likelihood that English interest rates will exceed those on his own currency. As Bristow J. remarked in *Miliangos (No. 2)* when the case was referred back to him by the House of Lords for determination of the amount of interest to be awarded

In my judgment the approach in English law should be: if you opt for a judgment in foreign currency, for better or for worse you commit yourself to whatever rate of interest obtains in the context of that currency.

This seems to be the correct solution, since the plaintiff would otherwise be 'overcompensated'. A person kept out of Swiss Francs foregoes the opportunity to invest in Swiss securities at Swiss interest rates. In order to take advantage of higher interest rates prevailing elsewhere the Swiss investor would have to open himself up to the likelihood of falling exchange rates and there seems no reason why the law should enable plaintiffs, at least notionally, to engage in financial dealings on terms that are more attractive than those which would be available in the marketplace.

The two aspects of financial market behaviour over the last twenty years that have made the question of the choice of interest rate particularly important have been first the greater volatility of exchange rates (and the associated greater spread of interest rates between countries) and secondly the increasing absolute level of interest rates. As interest rates get higher, so the proportion of a claim in contract or tort represented by interest also rises. By 1980 for example interest rates in both England and the US had risen to somewhere near 20 per cent annually. If a delay of several years attends the resolution of a case, this may result in the interest component of an award coming to represent a major proportion of the award itself, and in such circumstances it is important to award interest at the right rate.

A recent illustration of the contribution that interest may make is to be found in *BP Exploration Co (Libya) Ltd v Hunt* [1979]. The decision of the Court of Appeal, subsequently upheld by the House of Lords, was that Hunt should pay BP principal sums of US$ 10,801,534 and of £5,666,399. In addition, interest (calculated as from June 14, 1974 to the date of judgment, June 30, 1978) was to be paid upon the two principal sums in the amounts of US$ 4,774,289 and £3,060,219 respectively. Interest thus accounted for an additional 44 per cent and 54 per cent respectively on the principal adjudged payable.

TABLE 9.1 INTEREST RATES AND EXCHANGE RATES IN GERMANY
ENGLAND, USA AND SWITZERLAND 1961 – 80.

Year	Spot exchange rates[1]			Interest rates %p.a.[2]			
	$/£	SF/£	DM/£	UK	USA	Switz	Germany
1961	2.808	12.120	11.223	6.0	3.0	2.0	3.0
1962	2.803	12.104	11.204	4.5	3.0	2.0	3.0
1963	2.797	12.067	11.117	4.0	3.5	2.0	3.0
1964	2.790	12.039	11.096	7.0	4.0	2.5	3.0
1965	2.803	12.102	11.227	6.0	4.5	2.5	4.0
1966	2.790	12.073	11.097	7.0	4.5	3.5	5.0
1967	2.406	10.407	9.623	8.0	4.5	3.0	3.0
1968	2.384	10.258	9.536	7.0	5.5	3.0	3.0
1969	2.401	10.366	8.858	8.0	6.0	3.75	6.0
1970	2.394	10.331	8.732	7.0	5.5	3.75	6.0
1971	2.553	9.993	8.343	5.0	4.5	3.75	4.0
1972	2.348	8.862	7.517	9.0	4.5	3.75	4.5
1973	2.323	7.536	6.280	13.0	7.5	4.50	7.0
1974	2.349	5.965	5.659	11.5	7.75	5.50	6.0
1975	2.024	5.302	5.306	11.25	6.0	3.0	3.5
1976	1.702	4.173	4.022	14.25	5.25	2.0	3.5
1977	1.906	3.812	4.012	7.0	6.0	1.5	3.0
1978	2.035	3.296	3.719	12.50	9.5	1.0	3.0
1979	2.224	3.514	3.851	17.0	12.0	2.0	6.0
1980	2.385	4.200	4.672	14.0	13.0	3.0	7.5

Notes: 1 Market exchange rates as at the end of each year
2 Discount rate (or Bank Rate) as at the end of year
Source: International Financial Statistics, I.M.F.

Some idea of the differences between interest rates in different countries and of the associated movements in exchange rates may be derived from Table 9.1 in which appear interest rates and exchange rates over the last twenty years in some of the major trading countries. It is clear that in a country like Switzerland, interest rates have always been low and the currency powerful, whilst the reverse is true for countries like the UK.

Simple as the underlying argument might be, and clear though the judgment in *Miliangos (No. 2)* seems to be, there have been cases in which the interest rate applied by the courts has been different from the one prevailing on the currency in which judgment has been given. A good example of this is to be found in the Helmsing case. In *Helmsing Schiffahrts G.m.b.H. v Malta Drydocks Corp.* [1977] the plaintiffs were German shipowners who contracted through the second and third defendants for the building of two ships. The price was expressed in Maltese pounds, which had been agreed upon as the currency of account. Under the terms of the contract, the plaintiffs were entitled to a return of approximately 10 per cent of the purchase price because they had chosen not to order certain optional fittings. This sum, which amounted to 105,000 Maltese pounds, should have been paid to the plaintiffs in 1972 but was not actually paid until 1976. As a result of this delay the plaintiffs had to borrow money in Germany at German commercial borrowing rates, which were said to be approaching 15 per cent per annum at that time.

Kerr J. thought that the plaintiff's claim for payment in Maltese pounds was justifiable, but he decided to differ from the rule which Bristow J. had adopted. He held instead that over the period in question the plaintiffs were entitled to interest payable in Maltese pounds, but calculated according to prevailing commercial borrowing rates in Germany. Certainly the case before him was more complicated than the *Miliangos* case in that the currency in which judgment would have been made, that is Maltese pounds, was not the plaintiff's currency. It might be argued however that Kerr J. erred in the procedure that he followed in his calculations.

There are two ways in which the amount due to the plaintiffs could be logically calculated. The first entails the assumption that the plaintiffs, had they received the money due when it became payable, would have held it in an account in Germany. Had they done so, or been treated as having done so, the appropriate procedure would have been to convert the sum payable in 1972 in Maltese pounds into German currency at the exchange rate ruling at that time, and to then apply German interest rates for the period 1972 to 1976 over which the plaintiffs had been deprived of the use of the funds. The second possible line of argument is based upon the assumption that the funds would have been held in an account in Malta over the period in question. In this event the calculation would have proceeded by applying Maltese interest rates over the period to the basic sum expressed in Maltese pounds. The amount of principal and interest could then have been converted, if required, into German currency at the rate prevailing at the time of judgment. The method of calculation followed by Kerr J. conformed to neither of these two methods, but represented what has been described elsewhere as a 'conceptually-unsatisfactory hybrid' (Bowles and Whelan, 1979). By continuing to express the basic sum in Maltese pounds while applying German interest rates, the influence of the change in the exchange rate between the currencies over the period is suppressed.

CONCLUSIONS

The change in the law entailed by the *Miliangos* case and later decisions has a number of implications. We have in this chapter explored already some of the technical ramifications of the change. There are however other implications of the change, in particular for the question of the relation between the law and the commercial community to which we have not yet alluded. The change represented by the Miliangos decision is warmly welcomed by some commentators. Riordan (1978) for example claims that:

To trace the juridical development of this new rule reveals a most enlightening example of two key tenets of the reform and modernization process of the common law: first, that the law should reflect the fundamental (commercial) realities of the day, and second, that the judge has a major role to play in keeping the law in step with those realities.

Others have been less confident of the wisdom of the change. We have outlined some of these doubts earlier in this chapter.

Elsewhere, Lord Simon, in a dissenting speech in the *Miliangos* case, had raised an important question. He suggested that a change in the law as serious as the one approved by a majority of their Lordships in the Miliangos case might have undesired and unforeseen side effects. He remarked that: 'A penumbra can be apprehended, but not much beyond; so that when the search-light shifts a quite unexpected scene may be disclosed.'

Elsewhere in his speech he had suggested that a matter such as foreign money obligations demanded 'the contribution of expertise from far outside the law − on monetary theory, public finance international finance, commerce, industry, economics'. Although Mann (1976) has argued that this view may involve 'some slight exaggeration', it remains true that the House of Lords were making a revolutionary change and that many of the implications of the change were probably not fully appreciated at the time.

FURTHER READING

The law relating to tort and contract in an international context is in some respects complex and esoteric, as a brief glance at texts such as Shuster (1973), North (1979) or Mann (1971) will readily confirm. The great commercial significance of such law and of attempts to reform it have attracted remarkably little attention from economists and other non-lawyers, Bowles and Whelan (1981a and b) being modest exceptions. The Law Commission's recent working paper (Law Commission, 1981) on Foreign Money Obligations will in time be superseded by a full report, after which one may expect the Miliangos reforms to have been thoroughly worked through and settled. For further discussion see Mann (1971, 1976), Riordan (1978) and Knott (1980).

10

Regulation

The term 'regulation' covers a wide variety of legal (and other) machinery which is used to influence a wide variety of economic activity. We focus here on a rather narrow range of regulatory devices, namely those that are concerned either with imposing limits of various kinds on the actions that individuals or institutions can pursue or with preventing the exercise of monopoly power by private producers. This emphasis on the restrictive aspect of regulation may seem blinkered because, to take but two reasons, it ignores the use of regulatory agencies for constructive and facilitative purposes, and also because it ignores the important range of activities, particularly in the sphere of the provision of professional services, where self-regulation is of great importance. Without such a narrowing of the focus however the subject becomes unmanageable within the confines of a book of this kind.

Regulation is a device for influencing economic activity that operates alongside a number of others. To one side lies the tort system, which we have already discussed, under which individuals are able to take civil action against parties infringing their rights or failing to meet their obligations. To the other side lies full-blown public ownership (or nationalisation) under which government employees are appointed to manage enterprises and the government becomes the major or sole shareholder and decision-maker. The variety of activities that the term regulation embraces can be thought of as occupying a section of the spectrum which government intervention in the workings of society represents. In all of the instances with which we are concerned here, the object of regulation is to bring about an outcome that is different from the one which would emerge from the spontaneous operation of market forces. It is to be expected therefore that regulation occurs where, for one reason or another, we prefer an outcome that cannot be generated spontaneously. It seems natural therefore to begin by outlining some of the reasons why intervention suggests itself. We concentrate on those instances where some kind of market failure provides a rationale for a regulatory solution, although we point out also that regulation may represent a response not to some defect in the mechanism of market operation but be based simply on a judgment that a 'better' allocation and distribution of resources may result from appropriate intervention.

SOME MOTIVES FOR REGULATION

The list of motives we set out here should not be treated as either exhaustive or mutually exclusive, but simply as illustrative. We begin by looking at some of the barriers to the 'perfect' operation of markets that economists have identified. It is important to remember that provided that certain technical conditions are met, it can be shown that the unhampered operation of the processes of exchange and trade will lead to an allocation of resources that maximises social well-being, at least in the sense of ensuring that there will remain no reallocation of resources that would make someone better off without at the same time making someone else worse off. In the event of market failure this may no longer be true, although this is not *sufficient* to prove that some kind of regulation will necessarily give rise to a superior outcome.

Market failure

There are several sorts of difficulties that markets may encounter, and we look here at some of the ones which are most likely to be of relevance in the search for a rationale for regulation.

(i) MONOPOLY POWER

Regulation may first of all be directed at ensuring that monopoly power is not exploited to the disadvantage of society at large. Such control is generally exercised by agencies or authorities who have discretion to regulate activities directly or have powers to enquire into and prohibit certain actions. If a firm, or group of firms (a cartel), for example are thought to be exploiting their market power in such a way as to raise market price far above its competitive level then Anti-Trust regulations (in the USA) or Monopolies and Restrictive Practices provisions (in the UK) may be used. This may entail breaking up the firms involved, imposing a ceiling on the rate of return that is permitted, imposing direct controls on the price at which products may be sold and so on. It is not without irony that some regulatory activity includes various provisions that entail the deliberate creation of monopoly. Solicitors in the UK are a good example: they have a statutory monopoly of the right to charge for certain kinds of work, although the statute creating this right also lays down criteria designed to prevent the monopoly from exploiting consumers: for further discussion see chapter 12.

(ii) EXTERNALITIES

A quite different kind of regulation may characterise situations in which the object is to eliminate externalities rather than to limit monopoly power. Externalities prevail where individuals impose costs on others but are not made responsible for the fact. Regulation in the form of restrictions upon production levels, upon the range of inputs that can be used and upon the disposal of harmful waste products generated in the course of production may be designed to try and reduce externalities. That is to say that regulation may be used to put pressure on parties to move to an allocation of resources that lies closer to the one which is socially advantageous, even if this is at the expense of parties who were hitherto insulated from costs that they were creating.

This kind of regulation represents an alternative to the tax system and to tort. As was shown in chapter 2, externalities can be corrected, at least in principle, by imposing taxes that reflect the costs being imposed on others or by creating a tort action that 'internalizes' the externality by giving the party incurring harm an action against the party who is responsible for it. Provided that sufficient information is available and provided also that sufficiently accurate and penetrating control instruments are available, regulation represents a third way in which the optimal position can be reached. This regulatory approach to externalities will sometimes resemble the tax solution in that it entails imposing a requirement upon an individual and incorporates provision for a penalty (be it a fine or whatever) to be levied in the event that the requirement is not met. Such a 'tax' will generally take the form of being zero up to the permitted level of pollution, or whatever the relevant variable is, and positive beyond that point. Whether it increases steadily with the amount by which the approved ceiling is exceeded depends upon the context.

The two types of regulation identified thus far correspond with two forms of market failure. Abuse of monopoly power and the persistence of externalities are both sources of inefficiency in the sense that they prevent resources being allocated in such a way as to give rise to the greatest possible level of social welfare. Although some economists would argue that this is, of itself, far from being sufficient grounds for adopting regulation, there is little controversy about the inherent desirability of eliminating such inefficiencies insofar as it is technically possible and not overwhelmingly costly. Before we discuss this desirability in more detail, it is well to emphasize that there are many forms of regulation which cannot be rationalised in the way thus far discussed.

(iii) PRODUCT QUALITY

Regulation of product quality is very widespread. 'Products' here are to be broadly defined and to include all sorts of goods and services. The rationale for imposing minimum standards of quality on many kinds of product lies not so much in the fact that consumers themselves are incapable of ensuring that the good is of an adequate quality, but because it may be cheaper and more reliable to have the testing arranged by government inspectors than by consumers. Customers who buy new cars may not need to worry too much, since if the car should prove to be defective they can, because of the structure of contracts governing such sales, relatively easily insist that it be repaired or replaced. When consumers buy a new house however it may be a great deal more costly to seek remedies in the event of defects. The defects may take a long time to become apparent or it may be difficult to establish clearly that a defect is the result of the negligence of a builder, or *a fortiori* of a sub-contractor. Building inspectors, who monitor the construction of buildings as they are erected and who ensure they meet the extensive set of regulations incorporated in the Building Regulations, may be a relatively cheap solution to this problem. Reputable builders for example will welcome such regulations because they reduce the scope for 'fly-by-night' operators who build low quality housing only to disappear from the scene to go and trade in a different area or under a different name. House-buyers will welcome such a move because it reduces the extent to which they will feel obliged to commission elaborate surveys of the property, particularly if surveys are more difficult and thus costly to conduct after rather than during construction. This kind of regulation can thus be rationalised in terms of the search for ways of reducing transactions costs. Government agencies may be able to reduce the uncertainty which customers face at lower cost than could the consumers themselves acting alone. These kinds of arguments have been taken more seriously by economists since the publication in 1970 of an extremely influential article by Akerlof in which it was suggested that certain kinds of markets may collapse altogether if consumers lose confidence that product quality is being maintained.

(iv) MACROECONOMIC STABILISATION

The use of regulation for purposes of macroeconomic stabilisation is often observed, though less so under the more laissez faire economic policies of the 1980s than in previous decades. This kind of regulation is less often discussed in the 'law and economics' literature, even though it may be one of the more important ways in which legal regulation has a very direct influence on the way in which the economy behaves. The behaviour of financial institutions may have important consequences for the stability of money markets and stock markets. Although institutions like banks generally pursue prudent policies, there are regulations designed to prevent activities which may be suspected as being potentially destabilising. Later in this chapter we look very briefly at Exchange Control Regulations under which, until they were recently abolished, there were extensive restrictions on the ease with which United Kingdom citizens could obtain foreign currency and on the uses to which such funds could be put.

Non-market Grounds

In addition to the 'technical' grounds for regulation there are other motives which often precipitate calls for regulation. The two cases we distinguish here both entail demands for regulation that are the product of the view of some section of society that the spontaneous market solution is undesirable. The argument derives not however from a claim that there are factors preventing markets from functioning perfectly, but from a claim that the outcome of unrestricted market operation has unattractive characteristics.

(i) PRIVATE INTEREST

The first category of non-market grounds is referred to as 'private interest' because it entails pressure from a group or groups of individuals for the introduction of regulation. Often such pressure can be interpreted as an attempt by producer groups to introduce restrictions on suppliers of goods that are, or might be, rivals to their own. Such efforts are clearly directed at reducing the degree of competitiveness of such rival goods in an attempt to further the interests of the lobbying group. Quite how much regulation is best thought of as the result of such pressure group activity is difficult to say. In large part, the difficulty of identification results from the likelihood that the pressure groups involved will rely upon arguments that derive from market-failure type bases and as such may sound plausible. Many apparently monopolistic practices which receive protection from anti-monopoly regulation, for example, can be argued to derive from pressure from relevant producer groups. Restrictions on the provision of transport, communication and entertainment services for example are widespread and generally to the advantage of existing producers of such services and to the disadvantage of prospective producers and to the general public who will almost certainly have to pay higher prices for the services than they would do otherwise.

Pressure for the introduction of regulation of some kind will be commonly observed in markets where there are few traders (or 'oligopolists') who are anxious to coordinate their activities. By acting in concert they will generally be able to make higher profits than if they engage in competition with one another, and regulation may be one device that people in such a position can employ, or have employed on their behalf, to secure co-operation. Much regulation of the provision of professional services can be interpreted in this way as can 'closéd shop' agreements in many industries. Thus, whilst some regulation is directed at the control of monopoly power, there is some regulation which has been encouraged because it helps create and protect monopoly interests.

(ii) PATERNALISM

The second category of non-market grounds may often be difficult to distinguish from the first, at least in practice. The important difference in principle is that paternalism will normally refer to pressure from groups who do not stand to make a material profit themselves from regulation, even though they will prefer the outcome. The complete prohibition of sales of alcohol is perhaps the classic example of this although there remain many less spectacular instances such as the restriction of Sunday trading hours in the UK and restrictions on the use of dangerous drugs. Such restrictions reflect a view, which may not be universally shared, that to drink or to go shopping on Sundays are somehow activities that should be prevented. Having said that however it is important to note that the outlawing of discrimination on the grounds of sex, race or religion falls within this category. For all but the extreme libertarian, it is likely that most citizens approve of some such restrictions and disapprove of others.

THE CONSEQUENCES OF REGULATION

To the extent that different forms of regulation are directed at different kinds of problems it is not really possible to produce a simple description of the consequences of regulation. There are nevertheless a number of standard cases that can be readily documented. In this section we focus on two pieces of analysis: the first is concerned with the traditional case in favour of the control of monopolies and the second with the consequences of imposing regulation on markets in the form of price and associated controls. The object of such analysis is to try and establish whether there is anything in economic theory which holds clues about what the consequences of regulation are likely to be, for unless this can be clearly established, judgments about the wisdom of introducing or discontinuing regulation will be ill-informed.

The case in favour of controlling monopoly rests not just upon a desire to prevent the exploitation of consumers. Rather, it rests upon a desire to prevent the emergence of a situation in which the losses suffered by consumers exceed the gains made by producers. That there will be a net loss in aggregate terms is best illustrated by a diagram. In figure 10.1, a competitive industry will produce an output level of q_c and set a price of A. The characteristic of this solution is that price is equal to cost (assumed to be constant for all units of production) with the result that firms make zero profits. It should be noted in passing that costs here are defined to include a normal rate of return on capital employed so that the competitive firms are each doing as well as, but no better than, they would do if they were employing their resources in other sectors of the economy.

If the industry should now be monopolised, the

competition between firms that was responsible for maintaining price at the level A evaporates. The single producer is now able to adjust his price so as to take full advantage of demand conditions. It may be recalled from chapter 1 that producers will seek to set marginal revenue equal to marginal cost in order to maximise their profits. This will result in a rise in price from A to B in the figure and an associated contraction of output from q_c to q_m. At this new position the firm will be making profits over and above normal returns. These 'windfall profits' are measured by the rectangle ABDF, since the profit is AB per unit on each of AF units.

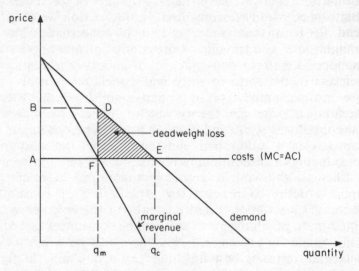

Figure 10.1 The Deadweight Loss from Monopoly

From the consumer's point of view, monopolisation has led to an increase in market price from A to B. This price rise means that some consumers will no longer buy the product whilst those who continue to buy it will have to pay a higher price. It can be shown that these consumer losses are measured by the area ABDE in figure 10.1, since 'consumer surplus' has contracted by that amount. Consumer surplus is given by the difference between the amount that a consumer would be prepared to pay for the good (represented by some point on the demand curve) and the market price he has to pay. On the first AF units that are sold the loss of surplus is AB per unit. Further losses are entailed by the fact that consumers of units FE at the competitive price do not find it worthwhile to buy at the monopoly price B.

The net loss, or 'deadweight loss' as it is generally termed, is given by the size of the triangle which remains when producer gains of ABDF are subtracted from consumer losses of ABDE. This triangle FDE is shaded in the diagram.

Whilst this analysis of monopoly seems to demonstrate unambiguously that monopoly is a 'bad thing' it is not without its critics. These criticisms, discussed at greater length in Rowley (1973), include the suggestion that costs will tend to be higher under monopoly than under perfect competition. The principal reason for this is said to be that monopolists, because they are relatively isolated from competitive pressures, will tend to be careless and to let costs rise more rapidly than they need do. This argument is weakened by the observation that monopolists will need to raise capital to continue or expand their activities, and the lower the profits they make the more difficult they will find it to generate funds either internally or through the finance market. Equally, if monopolists do not utilise their opportunities and resources fully, they will become vulnerable to take-over bids from other firms who think they could use the assets more profitably.

The control of monopoly is not the only kind of regulation with which we may be concerned. There are many markets in which government may well want to impose direct controls of some sort. These controls may include ceilings on the quantity traded, on the price charged or a specified minimum level of quality. Laws against discrimination on the grounds of sex, race or religion may also be added to the list. In many such cases, simple supply and demand analysis can be used to make inferences about the consequences of such regulation.

The regulation of housing markets, for example, may entail the creation of statutory, non-negotiable protection from eviction for tenants. Such restrictions on the terms on which property may be let will tend to reduce the supply of accommodation at any given level of rent, and thus will tend to force rents up. Attempts by government to prevent such rental rises, in the form of rent controls, will, as many elementary textbooks of economics (for example Lipsey, 1979, p. 441) point out, give rise to a shortage of such property since supply will tend to fall short of demand, as is illustrated in figure 10.2. The end result will thus be that tenants who occupy property at the time of the introduction of the controls will benefit, but prospective tenants will lose out because of the induced shortage of properties. This result is 'inefficient' effectively because tenants are being given more protection than they would want to 'buy' in a free market.

The question of the impact of regulation upon a market is, in the final analysis, an empirical one. To the extent that

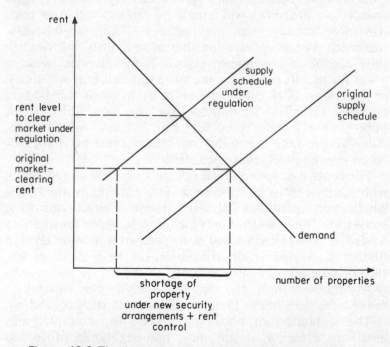

Figure 10.2 The Impact of Regulation on a Housing Market

governments from time to time change the pattern of regulation or intensify or weaken the degree of control they exert, there may be opportunities to test the assertion that regulation has one kind of effect or another. The difficulties associated with such testing are however formidable. Changes in other variables that occur as the regulatory changeover is itself taking place tend to obscure the true relationship between regulation and the state of some particular market. An attempt for example to establish the impact of sex discrimination legislation involves estimating the wage rates and unemployment rates that would have characterised male and female labour markets had the law not been introduced, and comparing these hypothetical conditions with those which were actually observed after the introduction of the legislation. Knowledge of the determinants of wage rates and unemployment is unfortunately inadequate for making very reliable estimates and, in conjunction with the fact that consumer prices and other variables may also need to be taken into account, imposes severe limits on the conclusions that can be reached about the impact of the legislation.

Different analysts draw different conclusions from these observations. Some will claim that the difficulties of empirical verification can be overcome with sufficient determination, and will pursue further empirical studies. Pollution studies are a good example of this. From a theoretical point of view, regulation is not a terribly attractive solution unless the costs of using the tort system are sufficiently high as to inhibit its capacity for controlling pollution. To their credit, several analysts concerned with pollution have made concerted efforts to establish how the level of pollution changed after the introduction of statutory controls or control agencies and to assess whether the increase in costs that firms encountered as a result of the controls were greater than or less than the benefits generated by the reduction in pollution levels. More commonly however participants in debate about regulation fall back on theoretical positions even though these very often require that unpalatable assumptions be made.

THE BEHAVIOUR OF REGULATORS

Irrespective of any merits that can be claimed for the outcome associated with regulation as compared with the outcomes following from other systems, some thought has to be given to claims that regulators will fail to pursue the goal of maximising net social advantage. The view that regulators, or at least the officials hired by regulatory agencies, will act in ways that are in the best interests of society at large is dismissed by many economists as naive. In the first place, it is naive because individual workers can normally be expected to pursue their own interests rather than those of the agency or firm for whom they work. The pursuit of individual ambition, better working conditions, more opportunities to take leisure during working hours are just some of the likely goals that individuals will have. The pursuit of such goals will of course be constrained in various ways, but many economists argue that these constraints will be more effective in the context of a private firm trying to maximise its profits than in a bureaucracy within a public sector organisation. Whether or not this is true, it is sometimes argued that regulatory agencies tend to go through a life-cycle. Whilst the agency may begin by putting into effect the wishes of government, in time it falls under the influence of producer groups whose interests it comes to pursue at the expense of either the public interest or the wishes of government.

More recent work (reviewed for example by Posner 1974) has rejected this simple 'capture' theory in favour of a more elaborate theory in which regulatory agencies may not just fall prey to producer interests, but may come under pressure from consumers and others. As Rowley and Yarrow (1981) recently expressed it, 'regulators are seen never to act as a perfect broker for a single interest group but rather to engage in cross-subsidization between competing interest groups in pursuit of a net political optimum as viewed in terms of potential voter support'. The same authors proceed to reject this theory, which is generally attributed to Stigler (1971), in favour of a model in which regulators set out to maximise their own utility in the light of the opportunities with which they are confronted by the reward/cost structures within the agency. In this kind of world, regulators will generally find it expedient to take decisions that make it likely that they will retain their position whilst at the same time not alienating the regulated group on the grounds that they represent a likely future employer. Amongst the implications of this theory is the likelihood that regulators will rely on policies that do not encourage entry of new competitors into a presently-regulated industry and may use policies that are consistent with the interests of powerful consumer groups, provided that such policies represent no real threat to existing profit levels.

The behaviour of government bureaucracies, and the motives of those who work in them remains an unsettled area in economics with the result that there is a lack of agreement about the extent to which regulatory agencies may be expected to conform to the wishes of those whose interests they are designed to reflect. The doubts that beset analysis of how effectively regulators pursue their tasks (or of how they select which tasks to pursue) thus compound the difficulties of establishing the intrinsic attractiveness of regulatory solutions as compared with tort or more direct forms of government intervention. If this all seems needlessly negative, it is important to recall that regulation is a very pervasive activity in many economies including the United Kingdom and the United States of America. The issues it raises are often complex but they do not go away just because one ignores them. It is curious that this object of such everyday importance has been relatively neglected not least because this is an area in which discussion can so obviously benefit from informed economic argument. Notwithstanding such criticism, there are areas of regulation about which relatively straightforward and (mostly) noncontroversial things can be said, and it is to some of these that we now turn.

APPLICATIONS

Taxi Markets

In both the United Kingdom and United States of America it is common for taxi markets to be regulated. Control usually centres first upon restricting entry into the market and secondly upon a price-fixing rule. In order to restrict entry, taxis are normally required to be licensed, it being illegal to operate unlicensed taxis either at all, or at least from certain specified picking-up points. A tariff of fares is usually specified as well, a premium being charged for carrying extra passengers or luggage or for journeys at certain times of day. The objectives of this regulation are presumably to ensure that cabs are available on 'reasonable' terms and that cab-drivers can be more easily induced under such arrangements to offer services of a quality that the public wants.

The consequences of regulation of this kind obviously depend upon the combination of the price and entry limits which are imposed. If price is set 'too low' then there is likely to be a shortage of cabs, and the entry quota will not be fully used up. If price is set 'too high', given the number of licences that the regulators are prepared to issue, then there will be an excess supply of people or firms wanting to supply taxi services. Impressionistic evidence suggests that in many instances it is this second situation which frequently prevails.

One indicator of price being 'too high' is the existence of a market on which licence plates are traded for considerable sums. The amount that prospective cab drivers will pay to enter the market will be governed by their perceptions of the extent to which their earnings in this market exceed those available elsewhere. The price of a licence plate can be interpreted as the capitalised value of the future monopoly profits to which it entitles the owner. Just like an equity share, or any asset for that matter, the capital value represents a future income stream that has been discounted at some appropriate rate. If traders in the market form the view that the policy of the regulators is about to change in some hitherto unsuspected way, then the capital value will change. Should taxi drivers think that policy towards fares will lead to a rise or fall in price then the value of their licence plates will go up or down respectively. The consequence therefore is that those who own licences when policy is shifted in favour of drivers will experience an overnight increase in the value of their assets. That is to say that the monopoly profits which are created by the existence of regulation will be appropriated by those lucky enough to have bought a licence when a limited number of them was initially issued or those lucky enough (or skilful enough) to have bought licences shortly before a change in policy.

The monopoly profits in question are earned at the expense of users of taxis who have to pay fares that are higher than they would be were the market competitive. Regulators can, if they exercise much cunning, appropriate these monopoly profits for their own agency. An annual auction of licences for example would enable the public authorities to exploit the competition between prospective taxi-drivers. Another method would be to make licences non-tradeable, so that anyone leaving the market would have to relinquish their licence and to charge a market-clearing price to those who wish to buy licences when they become available. In other words, by varying the pattern of rights that a licensee is able to buy it should be possible to ensure that any profits made at the expense of consumers are reappropriated by the regulatory agency. The other observation that one might make is that the regulatory agency can eliminate monopoly profits altogether if it is able to identify the combination of price and entry limits that would exactly match the supply and demand conditions which would prevail in a competitive market. Such a solution would be ruled out however because the premise on which regulation lies must surely be that the spontaneous market outcome has undesirable features that the regulators or regulations are designed to overcome.

It is important at this point to recall that monopoly entails a 'deadweight loss' and that even if regulation is set up in such a way that suppliers are not able to appropriate the monopoly profits themselves, the net result will be undesirable from an aggregate point of view. The regulator is able to act as a monopolist because he has control over the price at which the commodity is to be sold. If he chooses the price level and supply level that would be set by a firm that had a tight monopoly over all the taxis in the market, the deadweight loss involved will be given by the amount indicated in the discussion of section 10.2.

But this is not the end of the story: we have assumed in the analysis of the previous paragraphs inter alia, first, that the regulator acts as a conventional monopolist would and secondly that costs remain unchanged throughout. There are however reasons to suspect that these assumptions may need modification. The first reason for this is that there seems to be no clear reason why the regulators should raise the price to its monopoly level, since to do so is quite clearly to create an opportunity for suppliers to make profits without any advantage accruing to consumers that might offset the higher prices. If regulators raise price by less than AB, then the corresponding loss to consumers will be smaller as will the monopoly profits available to sellers. The second modification that might be relevant is that costs may rise under regulation.

The higher cost levels associated with regulation may arise from a number of sources. First, the legislation which enables the regulation may lay down standards of service exceeding those that would be offered in a competitive market: the granting of a licence may be contingent upon vehicles meeting standards of size, comfort and mechanical condition that exceed the standards which suppliers would offer under competition. In a competitive market, the quality of taxis would reflect the amount that consumers were prepared to pay for extra comfort or whatever. Under regulation, the regulators select (or at least have an influence over) quality.

The second source of cost increases under regulation results from decisions made by taxi-drivers themselves. Even though price is regulated there may be competition amongst licensed drivers for the existing business. This competition may be manifest in taxi-drivers being increasingly prepared to offer services at 'anti-social' times such as evenings or weekends. Costs rise here because we may assume that taxi drivers are offering to work at hours that they would not normally be prepared to sacrifice. The higher value to drivers of leisure at these times raises the opportunity cost of working. Competition between drivers may also be manifest in the provision of a superior quality of service. This may mean the installation in cabs of radios that raise the speed at which potential customers can be reached. It may also mean provision of more luxurious cars in the hope that this will attract customers away from other cabs. There are many possible variations on this theme: more courteous behaviour by drivers towards passengers, installation of air conditioning and so on.

The importance of competition between suppliers under regulation and the effect that this might have both on service quality and cost levels has been urged by various writers, very often in contexts other than taxi markets. The regulation of airlines is sometimes argued for example to have given rise to an excess provision of flights and excess quality in other respects of services. This is 'wasteful' in the sense that the regulators create conditions conducive to monopoly profits, some of which are then diverted into cost-raising efforts in the scramble for customers at the artificially high price. It might be re-emphasised that many contemporary economists argue that the raison d'être for regulation of product markets is generally producer pressure rather than a serious attempt to achieve greatest social advantage. Although consumers might appear to get certain advantages (like more comfortable taxis, or having to wait a shorter time to pay a lower price for a cab at night-time) they will have to pay a high price for these privileges.

This conclusion may however be ignoring some important dimensions of the problem. In the earlier part of this chapter it was suggested that there are various reasons why a freely-functioning market for a commodity may run into difficulties. The relevant arguments in the case of taxi markets may be that a licensing system protects consumers from rogue operators. Licensing authorities generally have powers to take action against licence holders who fail to satisfy set-down conditions. Should it be discovered that taxi drivers are not properly insured or are overcharging for example, their licence can be revoked or whatever. It would be much more difficult, it might be argued, in the absence of an effective licensing system, to identify and discipline drivers who exploit consumers. Certainly, this kind of argument is often used by those professions who have statutory powers to regulate their own members. There seems no reason in principle why taxi users as a whole should not welcome a system under which they pay a higher price in return for a greater degree of confidence in the quality of service they receive. It is of course impossible in practice to distinguish between regulation that seeks to protect the consumer from having his informational disadvantage exploited (or from having to negotiate the fare each time he wishes to take a cab) and regulation that is simply paternalistic. It is one thing to use regulation as a device for reducing the costs associated with making a transaction but another to intervene on the grounds that (at least some) consumers are incapable of striking reasonable bargains.

Exchange Control Regulations

Until 1980, it was illegal for private citizens of the United Kingdom to hold foreign exchange, and, if they wished to invest abroad they generally had to buy the requisite foreign currency at an artificially high price. The recent abolition of these controls provides a useful example of the consequences of relaxing a set of controls that had for a long time been regarded, at least implicitly, as an important device in stabilising the international value of sterling.

In a review of exchange control by the Bank of England (1967), it is noted that as early as the year 1299 there were restrictions on the import and export of currency into and out of England. Major controls had however been imposed at the start of the Second World War in 1939, there having been a widespread international growth in the use of exchange control during the financial crises of the early 1930s. The Bank of England (1967) described the object of the controls as being: '. . . to conserve and increase the gold and foreign currency reserves, and to ensure that they were used for the maximum national benefit'.

Without going into details, one of the main restrictions imposed by the controls was the existence of a limited pool of foreign exchange from which individuals wishing to acquire assets abroad were obliged to buy the foreign currency they needed. Currency could therefore only be acquired usually at a premium over the official exchange rate because the excess demand for foreign exchange kept its price 'artificially' high. When selling foreign assets investors had to sell 25 per cent of the proceeds of the sale at the official exchange rate, although they could sell the remaining 75 per cent back to the pool and thus recoup a part at least of the premium which they had paid when acquiring currency to buy the asset.

The arguments used in favour of exchange control were of two main kinds. First, by putting a premium on investment abroad it was hoped to encourage domestic investment. Investors had to use the pool not just when they were buying foreign assets for the first time, but also whenever they sold and bought them subsequently, with the result that the 25 per cent surrender rate would be applied each time and thus they forfeited at least part of any capital gain they might have made. The other argument in favour of exchange control was that under fixed exchange rates, exchange control helped stem an outflow of funds when sterling came under pressure on world markets. The move from fixed to floating exchange rates in 1972 weakened the second of these arguments, but it was a further nine years before the controls were abolished.

Although in the longer term investors would prefer to have the choice between investing domestically and investing abroad, those investors with existing foreign investments stood to lose if and when the controls were lifted. Two of the more virulent critics of Exchange Control Regulations pointed out, for example, that: '. . . The existence of a large body of investors liable to lose an appreciable proportion of their assets by the abolition of the investment currency premium is equivalent to a 100 per cent surrender of the premium and would be even more unpopular' (Miller and Wood, 1979, pp 66 – 67).

Nevertheless, Exchange Controls were abolished late in 1979. The consequences in terms of the shift in the balance of investment portfolios as between United Kingdom and foreign assets are difficult to establish after the event, just as they were difficult to predict before abolition. The suggestion was that immediately following abolition there would be a short period during which many United Kingdom investors would acquire overseas assets, but that this once-and-for-all adjustment of portfolios would relatively quickly give way to a new equilibrium that reflected the new terms on which investment abroad was possible. One commentator (Woolley, 1974) had estimated that the outflow of portfolio investment funds would be somewhat in excess of £3,000 million in the first few months after abolition. In a recent article, the Bank of England (1981) have made known their own estimates of the impact of removing the controls. These estimates seem to confirm that events took very much the predicted form even if some of the effects have been spread over a longer adjustment period than had been anticipated. Outward portfolio investment increased rapidly through 1980 and 1981. A finer breakdown of the figures shows that pension funds raised the proportion of cash flow placed overseas from 7 per cent prior to the abolition of controls to around 25 per cent in the latter part of 1981. Insurance companies, the other group of financial institutions through which a large amount of private sector portfolio investment is made, raised their acquisitions of overseas assets from 4 per cent of total acquisitions to 17 per cent over the same period. In both cases however this switch towards foreign assets was at the expense of holdings of British government securities rather than of holdings of UK company securities.

The arguments in favour of regulating foreign exchange movements seem, if anything, to be more ephemeral than those applied in the case of regulating markets for everyday goods and services. It is naive to characterise exchange control regulation as really protecting the public interest. Movements in exchange rates and rates of return are the devices which will protect domestic investment: foreigners will be keen (other things being equal) to invest in the United Kingdom if sterling is very cheap just as will domestic investors who find the costs of buying foreign exchange to invest abroad prohibitively expensive in such circumstances. If sterling should strengthen, United Kingdom investment becomes less attractive both to domestic and foreign investors. A consistent overvaluation of sterling under fixed exchange rates could, it is true, have threatened investment in the United Kingdom. Equally, before the floating of the pound, speculative flows of 'hot' money into and out of London occurred and it is perhaps easier to understand why controls came to be retained in such circumstances than in the conditions prevailing after the floating of sterling.

CONCLUDING REMARKS

Taking a rather narrow view of what constitutes regulation we have in this chapter identified some of the motives that may prompt regulation and looked at some of the ways in which it may affect the behaviour of relevant markets. Efforts to control monopoly power have long been a concern of economists. In recent years, developments in economic theory have opened the way for a broader range of regulatory activities to be analysed more convincingly.

Having said that, it should be emphasised that many economists are strongly of the opinion that intervention in markets is often misconceived and inappropriate. The principal grounds for this view are that regulatory alternatives may themselves be subject to 'failure' and that to demonstrate the superiority of regulation over spontaneous market outcome will often be much more difficult than is generally imagined. This view is based both on arguments that regulatory solutions are often inefficient even if properly implemented and also that, like other government agencies, institutions set up to administer regulation will, at least in part be isolated from pressures to behave efficiently and in ways that are consistent with the objectives that they are set.

How seriously this anti-regulation view should be taken is indeed a very controversial matter. Our aim here has been chiefly to articulate the kinds of reasons for which regulation might be introduced and to look at some of its effects. In many cases it is clear that a purely economic argument may fall short of being able to explain why regulation is as widespread as it is. Nevertheless one may surely claim that economic reasons are often advanced in discussion of regulation and that regulation has important effects on the economy.

FURTHER READING

Regulation is one area of law in which economists have traditionally had some interest. Much of this interest was directed at the questions of monopoly and competition policy: see for example Rowley (1973) or Swann (1979). Much recent work in this area has been concentrated on two areas. The first is the behaviour of firms which are subject to regulatory constraint, the seminal work being Averch and Johnson (1962) and later developments being summarised in Bailey (1973). The second of the two concerns is with the behaviour of regulatory agencies themselves, an interest triggered in part by the work of Niskanen (1971) on bureaucracies and in part by the increased awareness on the part of economists of the difficulties of ensuring that employees act in ways that are consistent with the objectives of the organisations for whom they work: this latter problem received pioneering treatment at the hands of Leibenstein (1966) and Williamson (1967) amongst others.

In addition to studies directed at the general problem of regulation, considerable empirical work has been done on the impact of regulation, particularly in the US. To give but a few examples one might cite: Rowley and Yarrow (1981) on the UK steel industry, Jarrell (1978) on the Electric Utility Industry in the US, Pyle (1974) on the regulation of interest rates in the US, Kitch, Isaacson and Kasper (1971) on the regulation of taxi-cabs in Chicago, MacAvoy (1971) on natural gas in the US and Peltzman (1973) on consumer protection legislation in the US.

11

The Economics of Ligitation

INTRODUCTION

Decisions about ligitation are an essentially practical matter. From an economic point of view they can be approached with the usual apparatus applied to decision-making under uncertainty, as we will show in this chapter. Although we will primarily be concerned with the decisions being made by plaintiffs and defendants in civil cases, much the same kind of approach can be used to look at decisions in the context of criminal law or regulation.

The public prosecutor, for example, has limited resources at his disposal and thus has to select which cases he is to pursue and with what intensity: see Landes (1971). In order to improve his record of convictions, the prosecutor may find it expedient to make deals with those who are being prosecuted and, for example, to offer to drop more serious charges if the defendant agrees to plead guilty to lesser ones. 'Plea bargaining', as this is called, is widespread in the United States of America, whilst controversy continues to surround the question of whether it occurs in the United Kingdom as well (see for example Baldwin and McConville, 1977 and Adelstein, 1981).

The same sort of logic applies in the case of regulation. Regulatory agencies with the responsibility of ensuring that various statutory requirements are met may often be in the position of not being able to monitor all prospective firms who might violate, or be violating, the rules. Accordingly, they have to make decisions about how to deploy their limited

187

resources and about the circumstances under which they will opt to take a case before the courts. Although agencies might often be reluctant to admit that they are not bringing the full weight of the law to bear upon all parties failing to fully comply with regulations, it is inconceivable in most instances that an agency will have sufficient resources to be able to guarantee 100 per cent compliance with the rules or to bring every known incident before the courts.

In the civil context with which we are concerned here, it need hardly be emphasised that the great bulk of cases are settled before a court hearing takes place. Very often therefore the relevant question will not be whether to press a claim or not but rather to identify the stage at which it is worthwhile agreeing to settle. When one comes to analyse these sorts of issues some important findings emerge: some parties are likely to be more persistent than others; legal advisers may sometimes have an incentive to encourage a client to settle at a stage other than the one which is in the client's best interests; the rules governing which party is responsible for paying the costs of a court hearing may have an important influence on decisions to settle out of court and so on. These sorts of findings are best reached by beginning with a model of how a party decides whether to pursue a claim.

THE DECISION TO LITIGATE

It is possible to think quite generally about the decision facing a party about whether to proceed any further with a claim at any stage in a claim's history. In essence, the party will have to compare the costs of going further (which may be high or low) with the benefits from so doing.

It is important to note that the question of how much a party might already have 'invested' in the claim will be irrelevant. Any costs that have already been irrevocably incurred are *sunk costs* and should be of no further concern. Suppose for example that a person has already accumulated a legal bill of £10,000 and has been offered £8,000 in full settlement. The fact that to settle now involves a 'loss' of

£2,000 is of no consequence when deciding whether or not to proceed. If the next round of negotiations will add £1,000 to the legal bill, it will be worthwhile to pursue the matter if and only if there is a good prospect of the offer rising by more than £1,000 as a consequence. To proceed, that is to say, is wise only if the net *additional* profit will be positive. It does not make sense to continue just because there is a prospect of receiving a higher offer: the party must be persuaded that the higher offer will more than offset the additional costs. If we seem to have laboured this point somewhat it is because of the frequency with which mistakes of this kind occur.

The reader may already be worried by a number of things: why haven't we as yet referred to the questions of liability and quantum, what happens if the outcome of the next round of negotiations is unknown, what happens if the party wants to avoid taking unnecessary risks and so on? These are all important questions, but can all be at least partly answered by refining the decision rule, or more technically the 'stopping rule', of the previous paragraph.

The main characteristic of negotiations of the kind we are describing is that each party to a claim cannot predict with any very great degree of certainty the position that the other party perceives itself to be in, and thus cannot predict how the other party will respond to offers. All of these arguments are of course equally valid for both parties to a claim: defendants have to make decisions about how much to offer on successive rounds just as those pressing claims have to decide when to accept an offer. In any event, it is important at this juncture to find a way of formalising uncertainty.

Both sides will have views, however difficult it may be to get them to quantify them, about two matters. First, the parties will have formed a view of the outcome that might be expected if and when the matter is referred to a court. This view will usually take the form of a series of possible outcomes to which are applied various probabilities rather than a single figure. If we ignore costs for the moment, the view may for example be encapsulated in an assertion of the kind: 'we have quite a strong case, but there's some chance that the claim will be reduced because of contributory negligence'. Thus there are three possible outcomes associated with taking the case to court: an award of zero if liability is not proved, a full award (of we assume, a fairly predictable size), and an award that is some proportion of the full award. Let us suppose that the relevant figures are zero, £50,000 and £30,000 respectively. At this stage the party will have also to assign a probability to each of these outcomes. These probabilities must add up to one, since all the possibilities are defined and are thus mutually exclusive. Let us presume that the legal adviser is well experienced and is able to assign probabilities of 0.2, 0.5 and 0.3 respectively. That is, there is taken to be a 1 in 5 chance of failing to establish negligence, a 50:50 chance of an award of the full amount and a 3 in 10 chance of a reduced award.

The *expected value* of the court award, EV, is given as the sum of the possible outcomes weighted by their respective probabilities: that is:

$$EV = 0 \times 0.2 + 50,000 \times 0.5 + 30,000 \times 0.3$$
$$= \quad 25,000 + \quad 9,000 \quad = £34,000$$

Following the terminology introduced in earlier chapters, we can say that a risk-neutral plaintiff would settle this case for any amount in excess of £34,000. Most plaintiffs however, might settle for rather less than £34,000 simply to avoid the uncertainty surrounding the amount that a court will award. An offer that seems rather modest, even as low as £20,000 for example, may seem awfully tempting, since it entails no risk. In any event we could, at least hypothetically establish the *certainty equivalent* for which any given plaintiff would settle. In the face of the prospect offered by going to court, the certainty equivalent is the amount that would leave the plaintiff indifferent between taking and leaving the offer. The difference between the expected value and the certainty equivalent is called the *risk premium*, R. This premium will be different for different parties but will be of considerable significance in determining the size of an offer to settle a defendant will make and the plaintiff's response to it.

From the plaintiff's point of view, the best strategy is to try and give the defendant the impression that he will settle only for an amount that is close to the expected value of the claim. If the defendant correctly guesses that the plaintiff is very averse to taking risks, he may exploit this information by offering much smaller sums in settlement than an 'objective' view of the facts of the case might suggest. In order to appear relatively indifferent about risk the plaintiff may attempt to give the impression of being rather more reckless and prone to gambling than others. This he may do by rejecting at least the first offer to settle by which he is tempted.

In practice, the size of the sums at stake, the fact that many defendants are insurance companies who are very experienced in handling claims for damages and the fact that many plaintiffs have little or no experience of the unfamiliar procedures and tactics may all combine to induce plaintiffs to settle for sums that are far below the actuarial, or expected, value of their claim. The same sorts of factors, as we suggested in the earlier chapter on the tort system and personal injuries, may inhibit many individuals who suffer harm from ever approaching a solicitor and taking action of any kind to recover damages. Equally, solicitors who are inexperienced in handling such claims on behalf of plaintiffs may even find themselves rather intimidated by the prospect of taking on experienced defendants who have a great deal of specialised knowledge on their side.

SETTLEMENT VERSUS TRIAL

Thus far, we have been treating reaching settlement as being rather like the process of negotiating to buy an item in a market where prices are not fixed and buyers haggle with traders. Buyers start by making low bids, sellers respond by offering high prices and so begins a process of negotiation which may end with the buyer going away empty-handed or with the sides reaching a bargain with which they are both happy. An important difference between bargaining in the market for a commodity and reaching an agreed amount to settle a claim for damages is that the very act of bargaining is rather more costly in the latter than in the former.

It is probably fair to argue that the main costs associated with pursuing a claim for damages tend to come in lumps, but may at different stages be very high. To oversimplify rather grossly, in the early stages there is the preliminary task of establishing the sequence of events leading up to the damage at issue, of establishing whether the prospective defendant was liable and of quantifying the damage incurred. This task may be simple or complex, and costs at this stage will be accordingly low or high. If the matter is not settled quickly, then it will be necessary to collect together the necessary evidence and to prepare for the possibility of a trial. Once this has been done, costs may be relatively limited until a trial actually takes place. This final stage is likely to be very costly indeed, and one or other of the parties will find himself paying the bill. The parties will generally therefore be anxious to find ways of avoiding having the case actually come to trial. There are various ways in which the proportion of cases coming to trial and thus costs can be kept down.

The first and most obvious comment to make is that whatever rules govern the assignment of legal costs between the parties, the party confronted by the likelihood of having to pay the trial costs will be very anxious to avoid a trial and will adjust his offer to settle (or his decision to accept an offer) accordingly. Settlements at the 'door of the court' enable a ·significant proportion of counsel's fees to be avoided whilst at the same time assuring each party that any offer made at that stage is unlikely to be a bluff, since it is a 'last chance' to settle. It should be mentioned that settlement at this stage might not just reflect the costs of a trial. The identity of the judge who is to hear the case may have a bearing on the views that the parties to the case take about the likely outcome of the hearing; counsel for the two parties may have private discussions and agree between themselves about the likely outcome (previous negotiations having taken place at arm's length) or it may simply be that one or other of the parties gets 'cold feet' and either accepts a previous offer should it still stand or increases the offer made to the other party. In addition to the cost pressures on parties to settle, there may be aspects of the lawyer/client relationship or of the cost rules that exert an independent influence. Such influences tend to be different as between countries, but are in any event a matter to which we return later in this chapter.

It is worth stressing that whatever steps are taken to facilitate early settlement, there will always be certain sorts of case that are most likely to end up in court and other sorts that will invariably be settled at an early stage. Amongst the ingredients for quick settlement may be listed the following:

(i) The parties take very similar views about the likely outcome of a court hearing of the case, or the plaintiff takes a pessimistic view;

(ii) The plaintiff is more averse to taking risks or is more impatient than the defendant;

(iii) The costs of a trial are high in relation to the amount of damages at stake;

(iv) The parties are represented by lawyers who are anxious for an early settlement.

As one might expect, the ingredients for most cases that go to trial include plaintiffs being prepared to take risks, and plaintiffs taking more optimistic views of their prospects of success. In addition, the more quickly that trials can be scheduled and the lower the costs of holding them, the more likely that any particular case will be decided by a court hearing rather than being settled beforehand.

From a policy point of view it may be noted that the long delays often associated with waiting for a case to be heard will tend to encourage settlement before trial. This tendency can however be offset in various ways. First, if adequate interest payments are included in damage awards to compensate for the delay in hearing the matter, then plaintiffs may be more inclined to wait. Secondly, if there is provision for either a preliminary hearing or for interim awards to be made to plaintiffs, then again there may be a greater number of cases that reach a hearing. A government concerned about such matters has various courses open to it. If it is thought that 'too many' cases are coming to trial, steps may be taken to change the statutes governing the interest rates payable or to change the availability of interim awards.

It is tempting to think that reducing delays in court hearings might influence the number of cases being set down for trial. Careful thought shows however that this probably will not be so. Provided that the parties still take a similar view about what the outcome of the case will be when it is heard, then greater delay should not of itself influence the number of cases being set down for trial. If plaintiffs do not like this greater delay, and defendants know that this is the case, then the sums offered to settle before trial will be lower than they were when delays were shorter. But the likelihood that the case will reach a court hearing will be unaffected. The defendant that is to say, is able to exploit the plaintiff's desire to have the matter decided quickly. Note that our argument does not require that the parties take the same view of the likely outcome of a trial that takes place in five years time as compared with one that takes place tomorrow. If both parties believe that the claim is more likely to be dismissed at a later hearing than an earlier one, because of the greater likelihood that witnesses will have disappeared or whatever, the likelihood of the case being set down for trial will probably be unaffected. What is important is whether the parties diverge in their views, not whether their views are influenced by the remoteness in time of the trial.

THE SIZE OF SETTLEMENT

Having argued that the plaintiff's decision about whether or not to go to trial depends upon some factors but not upon others, we look more carefully now at the size of offers made by defendants. It has already been pointed out that any offer to settle may be influenced by the defendant's own attitude towards risk. It has been implied that the rules about the assignment of legal costs, about the interest rate payable and the availability of interim awards are also factors that will be germane to negotiations. We take up now the influence of rules about interest rates, and of any differences between the interest rate applied by the courts and

    (i) commercial interest rates;
    (ii) subjective discount rates.

The first point to make is that if the interest rates awarded in damages as compensation to plaintiffs for being deprived of the use of the funds whilst the case is being resolved lie below prevailing market rates this will favour defendants. The reason is obvious: the defendant is effectively borrowing funds from the plaintiff between the date when the harm occurred and the date when payment of damages is finally made. If this borrowing is cheap, the defendant will be keen to hang on to the money for as long as possible. Equally, if the borrowing is expensive, the defendant may be more anxious to settle. The easiest way to establish whether borrowing is cheap or dear is to ask what the defendant could do with the money. At worst, the defendant can set aside an amount of his liquid funds in a risk-free investment such as a building society account or a short-term government security. If such investments earn him more than the rate at which interest is charged on the damages that he will have to pay sooner or later to the plaintiff, then he will delay. The value of such benefits can however be readily calculated, and the defendant will be persuaded to settle only if he is 'compensated' for having to forego such benefits. Thus, the lower the interest rate charged by the courts on damages, the lower will be offers to settle out of court, other things being equal.

There are in this regard some important criticisms that one can make of English practice. In the first place, the law was slow to respond to the increase in the level of interest rates generally that occurred in the course of the 1970s. Statutorily-determined interest rates were varied only after a considerable delay, and many plaintiffs must have suffered heavily. More fundamental however is the explicit refusal of English courts to offer compound interest rather than simple interest. This refusal has deleterious consequences for plaintiffs that are sharply accentuated in times of high nominal interest rates: see Bowles and Whelan (1981c).

Interest is awarded under the Law Reform (Miscellaneous Provisions) Act of 1934. The relevant section of the Act expressly forbids the awarding of 'interest upon interest' and thus effectively rules out the award of compound interest.

Particularly in commercial cases where very large sums may be at stake, it is very difficult to justify the retention of a 'simple-interest only' rule. The Law Commission (1978) have recently reviewed this question and found no compelling reason to seek any changes in the existing rules, so that it seems unlikely that a switch from simple interest rates will be forthcoming in the foreseeable future. It is nevertheless interesting to examine the implications of refusing to allow plaintiffs to claim amounts of interest that can be regarded as sufficient to restore them to the position which they would have been in had the tort or breach of contract or whatever not materialised. As in previous sections it will be shown that the end result will be further downward pressure on the sums offered by the defendants in out of court negotiations.

Anyone who has ever saved anything will know that any interest earned on a savings account will normally be credited back to the account rather than despatched to the saver. The frequency with which such interest payments are calculated varies between institutions: in the case of very large commercial accounts it may be every day whilst in the case of small private savings accounts it may be quarterly or less frequently. Either way, if the account is held for three or four years at a time when interest rates are high the sum of money standing in the account at the end will be considerably greater if interest payments are based on compound rather than simple rates. Suppose for example that I have £100 today in 1981 which I put into an account offering an interest rate of 10 per cent, and that sums are compounded on an annual basis. Over the next four years, this sum will grow to £146.41 provided that the interest rate remains constant. If interest is calculated at a simple rate over the same period, the sum at the end would be £140, since £10 will have been added to the principal at the end of each of the four years. Now it may seem that the difference in the amounts generated under the two schemes is rather small, since £6.41 represents only a rather small fraction of the total sum involved. But, looked at another way, £6.41 represents about 14 per cent of the interest payable under the compounding procedure. When very large sums are at stake, and in commercial cases, millions of pounds may be involved, such a proportion may correspond to a large sum of money. Note that if the calculation is done with interest being compounded more frequently the difference is even greater. If for example the institution calculates the interest payable quarterly, the £100 will have become £148.45 after four years with the result that the loss from using simple interest rates as compared with compound rates rises to 17.4 per cent of the amount of interest payable.

It is not at all clear why plaintiffs should be consistently penalised in this way. There are some circumstances in which it may be tempting, but wrong, to think that it is appropriate to apply simple interest rates. Suppose for example that we consider a case of a judgment debt: A promises to pay B for a consignment of potatoes. The goods are delivered as arranged, but A fails to make payment. B then seeks to recover the money from A plus some element to cover having been kept out of his money. In the interim, B increases his bank overdraft in order to finance his normal operations. If for simplicity, the contract price was £100 then it may seem that the cost to B of being kept out of his money is best calculated at simple rates, since we are concerned only with the cost of servicing the increased debt of £100. At an interest rate of 10 per cent per annum this implies that A should receive £10 from B by way of interest for each year that the debt was outstanding. This argument, needless to say, is incorrect.

If we compare the size of B's overdraft having been kept out of his money with the size that it would have been had the money been paid as agreed, it will be clear that compound rather than simple rates are appropriate. B effectively has to borrow money to pay the extra interest on his overdraft and such borrowings will in their turn have to be paid for in the usual way. If interest is calculated quarterly, the initial increase of £100 in the overdraft will appear an excess of £148.45 after four years. By contrast, if the court awards interest at a simple rate of 10 per cent then B will ultimately recover only £140 after a four year lag. Exactly the same result emerges if instead of arguing that B had had to increase his overdraft, he had simply had a smaller amount of capital available for working capital or investment purposes. The losses would be calculated as the investment opportunities foregone, and thus by the sum that would have been generated had the funds been available to the plaintiffs.

The use of simple interest rates seems to work unambiguously against plaintiffs. Offers to settle are depressed because both sides know that interest payments will be lower than would be required to meet adequately the requirement of *restitutio in integrum*. But it should also be noted that not only will settlements reflect the fact that the amount that a court will award is lower than in some sense it 'ought' to be. It will in addition reflect the fact that defendants have an incentive to delay reaching a conclusion to the case. So long as defendants can 'borrow' from plaintiffs at simple interest rates rather than at the compound rates that commercial lenders will ask, they will want to delay settlement as long as possible. Plaintiffs can of course circumvent the delay by taking a lower sum in settlement, but defendants will be able to exploit this impatience in the usual way. Putting the point another way, plaintiffs will realise that defendants can benefit from the application of simple rather than compound rates both by virtue of the lower damage awards entailed and by virtue of the threat to delay proceedings which the defendant is likely to wield.

The other problem that arises when calculating the amount of damages that are to be awarded to compensate for the delay in resolving a case concerns the appropriate discount rate. It has been argued thus far that plaintiffs should receive compound rather than simple interest because this would more closely correspond to the market opportunities that they forego. There may be many plaintiffs however, for whom it would be appropriate to apply interest rates that exceed prevailing market rates. The sorts of interest rates used by the courts were, at least until the abolition in 1981 of Minimum Lending Rate, tied to a rate published by the Bank of England. This interest rate however was generally considerably lower than the rate at which private individuals or small companies could borrow. The use of measures such as a Central Bank discount rate will tend to understate the costs incurred by plaintiffs, because many plaintiffs will simply not have access to markets on which borrowing can be undertaken at the sorts of rate that will generally be fixed in a court judgment. An allied shortcoming of using a central bank discount rate is that individuals may place a greater premium on early receipt of money than is suggested by ordinary interest rates. Poor individuals in particular may simply find it impossible to borrow money and yet may be very desperate for funds if they have had an accident that further depresses their temporary earning prospects. For the courts to apply conventional market rates in such circumstances is grossly to underestimate the losses that plaintiffs experience from the delay associated with recovering damages. Unhappily, this is yet another instance where defendants are normally able to exploit the impatience or myopia of plaintiffs and offer lower sums in settlement.

PAYMENTS INTO COURT

Nowhere is the capacity for clever defendants to reduce their losses as clear as in the English system of payment into court. Under this system, defendants can pay a sum into court after being served with a writ. The plaintiff has the option of accepting this offer in settlement within 21 days or of proceeding to let the court hear the case. If, in the latter event, the court's decision is to award damages that are less than the sum paid in, then the plaintiff becomes liable to pay both his own costs and the costs of the defendant from the date of the payment-in onwards. Should the court award an amount of damages that exceeds the payment-in then the plaintiff has his costs met by the defendant in the usual way.

Whilst the intention of the payment-in system appears laudable enough, namely to encourage settlement and to reduce the caseload being handled by the courts, one of its main effects is to make life yet more difficult for the plaintiff. The main reason for this is that if the court awards more than the amount paid-in, the plaintiff is in the same position as if the system did not apply, whilst if the court awards less than the amount paid-in then the plaintiff is worse off than he would otherwise have been. There are again two components to the reduction in the size of the damage received by the plaintiffs. In the first place, even if the plaintiff wins he may have to pay some of the defendant's costs, but secondly there is greater uncertainty associated with the net amount with which the plaintiff will end the day in the sense that actual awards are now more widely spread around the average award. This will raise the amount that a given risk averse plaintiff will forego in order to avoid uncertainty and thus will reduce the size of the offer at which he will opt to settle. For further discussion of economic aspects of the payment-in system see Phillips and Hawkins (1976) or Phillips, Hawkins and Flemming (1975).

CONCLUDING REMARKS

From what has been said so far in this chapter, it seems that plaintiffs, particularly if they are risk averse individuals, may find litigation to be a difficult and unrewarding matter. Whilst one may dismiss this argument as sentimental it seems nevertheless to be quite an important one and one that has given rise to various proposals for reform, and indeed has prompted differences in practices between countries. In the following chapter in which we look more closely at the provision of legal services we investigate the contingent fee system. Under such arrangements, which are widely used in the United States of America for example, plaintiffs are able to shift many of the risks of litigation to their legal advisers. This effectively raises the value of claims to plaintiffs, because the legal adviser is generally better at absorbing risk than the plaintiff himself. It is interesting in this regard to observe the rather heavy involvement of trades unions in personal injury litigation in the United Kingdom. The legal departments of unions, because they handle relatively large amounts of litigation, tend to be quite expert at handling claims and in a good position to absorb risks. The provision of such services may be used as a powerful incentive to attract prospective members.

As far as litigation in the context of contract is concerned, some economists would argue that the prospect of difficulties confronting plaintiffs should not be taken too seriously. When parties sign a contract they are assumed to be familiar not only with the possibility that a breach may occur but also with the amounts of damages that they may expect to recover in the event of breach. If they are not happy with what they see, they may either insist upon clauses being introduced into the contract which makes more adequate allowance for the terms upon which damages are to be calculated or they may adjust the price payable under the contract. In charterparties for example it is very common for liquidated damages, in the form of demurrage payments, to be agreed when the contract is made. This allows the parties to specify the terms upon which delay is permitted and avoids the need for costly legal action each time such delay occurs. Equally, the trader who is unsure about whether a buyer will pay the price that he agrees under a contract may add a substantial premium to his asking price in order to compensate for the likely difficulties that he will experience should the buyer fail to pay. The more difficult and thus costly it is to recover debts, the greater will be this premium.

Another means of reducing the costs of settling disputes involves the 'streamlining' of some of the legal institutions and procedures. The use of arbitration and small claims courts are but two examples of ways in which cases can be settled far more quickly and conveniently than is possible in more conventional courts. Arbitration in commercial cases is conducted by specialists, parties agreeing at the outset that any disputes will be referred to an independent arbitrator, and his decision honoured. Any new points of law which are raised in the process of arbitration will normally be referred to the appropriate court. There is considerable variety both within and between jurisdictions in the kinds of ovations that have been made in the attempt to reduce the costs of resolving legal disputes and there can be little doubt that pressures for further ovations in this area will persist.

The final point we look at here is the proposal that in some circumstances plaintiffs be offered a premium for successfully pursuing a case. Phillips, Hawkins and Flemming (1975) argue that plaintiffs who fail to reach an out-of-court settlement should receive a bonus on top of their damages to offset the delay and uncertainty that they have had to suffer in waiting for the case to come before the courts. Since one may argue that cases actually heard have an exemplary value and will be used as a starting point in out of court negotiations in many subsequent cases, the object of the court should be to set damages at such a level that subsequent out of court settlements should reach what the court regards as an appropriate level. If for example out of court settlements are generally 20 per cent below the level that would be awarded by a court, then the court should award a 25 per cent bonus to successful litigants. This would ensure that in the vast majority of cases, out of court negotiations would bring the parties to reach agreement at the 'right' figure.

FURTHER READING

The importance of settlement before trial is not in dispute. Evidence to the Winn Committee (1968) indicates that less than 5 per cent of (civil) cases go as far as a court judgment. The great bulk of cases are resolved by negotiation between the parties, for reasons discussed in Tullock (1971). More recently it has become clear that some of the devices designed to encourage settlement prior to trial or to raise the speed with which settlement is reached, in fact tend simply to bias the level of settlements downwards: see Phillips and Hawkins (1976) and Phillips, Hawkins and Flemming (1975).

12

Economic Aspects of Legal Services

INTRODUCTION

The provision of legal services is a matter that has attracted considerable interest in recent years. Amongst the more persistent criticisms has been that legal services are very costly. This may be undesirable of itself because people may be expected to prefer cheap services to expensive services, other things being equal. More seriously perhaps, the high costs of legal services can be expected to impose severe limits on the access of the poorer members of society to the legal system. In this chapter we look at both these areas of controversy. We look also at the question of whether changes in the structure of the lawyer-client relationship may influence either the overall level of demand for legal services, or their accessibility to the less well-off.

The central focus of any economic analysis of the provision of legal services is bound to be the costs of such services. The most elementary observation is that if legal services are expensive, people will be reluctant to use them. There are however some areas in which non-legal services can be more readily substituted for legal services than others. House buyers know that unless they are prepared to do their own conveyancing they are likely to incur considerable expense in hiring a solicitor, but at present it is illegal for anyone other than a solicitor to charge for the provision of these essential services. At the other extreme there may be many trivial incidents that at least potentially form the grounds for taking legal action. In most of these cases the individuals affected will find some informal remedy rather than retaining professional legal services. There is however a large grey area where the demand for legal services will be sensitive to price, an area over which taking legal advice is but one of several options that an individual may consider.

Discussion of the provision of legal services generally involves two different types of argument, namely issues of efficiency and issues of distribution. From an efficiency point of view, it is important that the price of legal services should properly reflect the costs of providing them, since only in such circumstances will resources be sensibly allocated either within the legal sector or to the legal sector as against other sectors of the economy. From a distributive point of view the concern is to ensure that existing legal services are 'fairly' distributed.

Views about what constitutes a 'fair' distribution differ widely: some people will argue that willingness to pay the going market price is the best criterion for judging who should get legal services whilst others would argue that some notion of legal need is the prime concern, and so on. In the following sections we look at various aspects of the debate about the provision of legal services and try where possible to distinguish between the two elements of efficiency and distribution.

PUBLIC VERSUS PRIVATE PROVISION

Probably the most radical line taken in criticism of the existing systems in most capitalist or mixed economies is that the reliance upon private provision has the effect of restricting access to legal services to the well-off. Poor people with important legal problems or 'legal needs' as they are sometimes more emotively called are denied access to legal resources which are instead being used on 'flippant' matters by the wealthy. The demand for legal resources under the present system of essentially private provision is thus likened to the demand for health resources that would be thrown up if health services were privately provided. This analogy is in various respects a valid one: both health and legal resources are needed by rich and poor alike and it may be quite difficult to predict the occasions upon which any single individual will find himself wanting such services. In other respects the analogy is less valid: a socialised legal system would probably be more heavily used by the better-off who would have more at stake, and it might be questioned whether the effect of public provision might not thus be to subsidise the rich at the expense of the taxpayer generally.

The other major problem would probably be that whilst the rich might be over-represented in the groups to whom public legal services were provided, the overall level of demand that would be generated by lowering the price of legal services (or possibly subsidising them completely) might well come to exceed the volume of legal resources available. In the National Health Service, provision of health care at a zero price generates more demand than the system can cope with. This excess demand has to be filtered by a variety of devices: using general practitioners as gatekeepers to ensure that the flow of patients to see specialists remains manageable; using queues as a means of deterring people from wanting public treatment and so on. One can well imagine that lawyers would get snowed under with work and that elaborate mechanisms would have to be introduced that were capable of reducing demand, irrespective of whether these methods for discriminating amongst prospective customers met with general approval.

There is provision at present for selective subsidies to less well-off clients under the Legal Aid and Legal Advice Schemes. These schemes seem to attract a lot of criticism even though they seem on most criteria to represent a step in the right direction. Claims are sometimes made that the amounts that solicitors can recover under the schemes are so low that it is not worth bothering to operate them whilst at the same time occasional abuses are detected where it is clear that solicitors are devoting 'too much' time to cases because the fees are more attractive than those available from using the time in other ways. Equally, the decisions about which applicants are to be granted help are often criticised for being too harsh or for being uneven as between areas or uneven as between applications in different sorts of cases. Problems of this kind are very difficult to eliminate, just as experience with the structure of payments to doctors and dentists in the uneasy public/private divide in the health services would suggest.

Whatever the theoretical arguments about the relative merits of public and private provision, there is some evidence from the operation of law centres about the practicability of trying to widen the proportion of society to whom legal services are made available. The first law centre set up in the United Kingdom opened in North Kensington in London in 1970 and has since been followed by quite a number of others. These centres generate income from a variety of sources: from legal aid payments (just like private solicitors), from central and local government and from a variety of charities. The centres are located in poor areas and offer, in an informal way, legal services to individuals and often to community groups as well. As might be expected, the sorts of cases with which these law centres deal are often rather different from those handled by private firms of solicitors. Landlord-tenant disputes and housing problems rather than conveyancing provide a considerable bulk of the work, whilst employment, social security and consumer problems play a more prominent role than they do for most private firms. If the present political climate is rather unconducive to any expansion of such facilities, there seems little doubt that there does exist a significant potential demand for such services when they are provided on terms that poorer groups can afford.

Public involvement in this area need not of course be limited to financing the supply of legal services to the less well-off. In the 1970s when the consumer movement was at its most effective in the UK, some local authorities were providing information to consumers about the level of conveyancing charges being made by local solicitors. Such activities will tend to sharpen the degree of competition between providers of services and is likely to benefit the public in the form of lower prices. Equally, there are various statutes which either directly influence the level of legal charges or empower government agencies, such as the Taxing Authorities, to influence legal charges in particular instances. At the same time however it is only because of publicly-provided protection that the two parts of the legal profession retain their considerable powers. The prohibition of advertising by solicitors, for example, may enable certain wasteful activities to be avoided but does not necessarily operate to the public's advantage. Fees may be considerably higher as a result of the absence of advertising and the corresponding lack of incentive for solicitors to offer attractive prices.

CONVEYANCING FEES

Solicitors rely heavily upon conveyancing activities for both revenue and profits. Without the legal monopoly of the right to provide and charge for such services, the profession would probably be smaller and less profitable. This is not *necessarily* to say that the monopoly is a bad thing; such a judgment can only be reached by examining the alternatives carefully. Nevertheless, the fact that the Monopolies Commission, the Prices and Incomes Board and a Royal Commission have all been invited in recent years to examine the position does suggest that there is persistent concern about the possibility that solicitors as a whole are doing unjustifiably well out of their monopoly. Indeed there have been reforms instituted at different times that have attempted to control the profitability of such services, although many critics of the present arrangements would argue that the root of the problem, namely the statutory monopoly, remains. In the following paragraphs we look at some of the criticisms in more detail.

We begin by establishing the level of earnings from conveyancing as compared with earnings from other types of work. It should be said immediately that information about the earnings of solicitors (or of barristers for that matter) is not easy to find. This is in large measure because many solicitors operate in partnership and thus are obliged to disclose little if anything about their incomes and profits.

Although it is relatively easy to establish the salary scales of solicitors employed by public authorities, this is not very helpful when it comes to discussing conveyancing fees and so on, since conveyancing is generally done by solicitors in private practice. Most of the relevant information that is available derives from specially-commissioned surveys set up by the public bodies which have from time to time investigated solicitors' earnings.

The PIB report of 1968 and the survey conducted by the Royal Commission on Legal Services, whose report was published in 1979, both show a broadly similar picture of the importance of conveyancing for solicitors' incomes, as is clear from Table 12.1. Unfortunately, the Royal Commission's survey did not produce data about the profitability of conveyancing, and thus gives a rather less usefull overall view than the earlier Report. Nevertheless, a number of things emerge clearly: conveyancing accounts for a good proportion of income, particularly in smaller practices and practices located outside Central London. In addition, conveyancing seems from the Prices and Income Board to be highly profitable since it accounts for a much higher proportion of revenue than of costs. The Royal Commission's work 'did not provide good data on profitability . . . but tends to confirm the findings of the N.B.P.I. in 1966 that conveyancing is more profitable than most other classes of work' (Royal Commission, 1979, paras 16.170/1).

There are a number of points to bear in mind when looking at figures such as those in Table 12.1. In the first place, the method of charging for conveyancing was changed in 1973 following the NBPI Report, with the consequence that it may have been subsequently less profitable. Secondly, the volume of revenue generated by conveyancing fees depends upon conditions in the housing market, since in boom times a higher number of properties will be changing hands and property prices will be unusually high whilst the reverse will be true when property markets are in recession. Thirdly, the Table gives no indication of the relative profitability of conveyancing different sorts of property and there may be grounds for suspecting that the change in the system of charging instituted in 1973 may have affected the degree of cross-subsidisation taking place. Other more conventional caveats include the different kind of questionnaire used to elicit the reported information and the rather poor response of those asked to provide figures.

TABLE 12.1 DISTRIBUTION OF INCOME AND EXPENSES
ASSOCIATED WITH CONVEYANCING BY SIZE OF PRACTICE

(i) *Prices and Incomes Board*, figures for 1966.

size of practice	per cent of total income/expenses	
	income	expenses
1 principal	64.4	47.5
2 principals	61.4	45.6
3 or 4 principals	57.4	39.6
5 or more principals:		
(a) Central London	33.5	28.0
(b) Elsewhere	57.1	37.0
All practices	55.6	40.8

(ii) *Royal Commission on Legal Services*, figures for 1975/76

size of practice	per cent of gross fee income*
Sole practitioners	59.9
2 partners	56.2
3 – 4 partners	53.2
5 – 9 partners	47.8
10 or more partners	32.4
All firms	47.4

*no figures for costs (or profitability) available from the Royal Commission Survey.

The scale charges system

Over the period 1883 – 1972 the size of fee that could be

charged for conveyancing work was subject to a ceiling fixed by statute. The scale of fees was adjusted from time to time under the Solicitors' Remuneration Orders of 1919, 1925, 1944, 1959, 1963 and 1970. Fees were governed by the value of the property involved, higher valued property attracting higher fees. Pressure for a reform in the method of fixing scale fees mounted in the wake of the PIB Report in 1968 and culminated in the revision in the method of determining fees set out in the Solicitors' Remuneration Order 1972 which came into effect on January 1, 1973.

One of the principal criticisms of the scale fee system was not so much that fixed charges were of themselves a bad thing but rather that the scale was unbalanced. In the Prices and Incomes Board Report it was suggested that fees were too high for high-valued property and too low for low-valued property. They noted:

It is quite clear that at the top end of the range conveyancing is exceptionally profitable while . . . conveyancing work at this level [below £1,000] is still unremunerative . . . We propose, therefore, to suggest certain increases up to £2,000. This suggestion . . . would be consonant with our general recommendation that charges should be related to effort required − the effort entailed being sometimes relatively greater for a less costly house − and should facilitate a more economic as well as a more equitable deployment of time. (para. 54).

This was not a contentious point as is readily confirmed by a Memorandum published around the same time:

Scale fees were introduced in 1883 and have since then been maintained on the basis of being geared to the monetary value, with the figures carefully graduated so as to ensure that the loss on the lower value transactions is compensated by the fees higher up the scale. (Memorandum of the Council of the Law Society, *Law Society Gazette,* May 3, 1972 at 386 para 12).

The Law Society can be interpreted to be arguing on distributive grounds that the bias in the scale of charges was to the benefit of the rich at the expense of the poor. The Prices and Income Board on the other hand is suggesting that resources would be more efficiently allocated if the fee charged was based upon the amount of work involved rather than the value of the property involved. It is instructive to spend a moment considering how the inefficiency of biased scale charges would be manifest.

If it is very profitable to conveyance expensive property then the most profitable practices will be those located in areas of high property values. These practices will find it easier to attract young solicitors. Elsewhere, conveyancing will be less profitable and solicitors will tend to move away from practices in depressed areas. If fees are fixed, any competitive forces will be felt first in the number of solicitors competing for business and secondly in the tactics that they use. Advertising is banned and thus non-price competition will not be very fierce. Although a concern to establish a good reputation may encourage solicitors to be careful and thorough with clients who are buying and selling expensive houses, solicitors may often enjoy what one might term 'windfall profits' when they are in an established position in an affluent area. This will mean higher incomes, the possibility of working fairly modest hours and the possibility (often eschewed it seems) of spending lavishly on offices. It will also mean that prospective partners will have to pay a high entry price to buy into a practice in these areas.

Conversely, practices in depressed areas will offer poor income prospects and will only be able to attract the less able or ambitious. The consequence is likely to be that the quality of legal services in depressed areas will be lower than it would be if the scale charged offered a more even return to work at different levels. It should be remembered also that the distribution of home ownership is uneven across the country. In working class areas there will be a higher proportion of people living in local authority housing, and this will contribute to the incentive for solicitors to locate themselves in wealthier regions.

There is however an irony in the developments following the move to replace scale charges by a more flexible system of determining fees, an irony that emerges when one looks at the judicial interpretation of the 1972 Order and at prevailing legal practice. Casual observation suggests that solicitors, if asked to give an estimate of the cost of a conveyancing transaction, will want to establish the value of the property before quoting a figure. When they send out the bill after the transaction has been completed, charges will be carefully itemised in such a way as to suggest that the cost reflects the volume of work that has been done and the amount of any relevant expenses incurred. If this practice seems to disappoint the hopes of the reformers responsible for the 'abolition' of scale charges it can at least boast a good measure of judicial support. In a case brought to establish how the 1972 Order was to be interpreted it became quite clear that the value of the property was to constitute a major criterion in fixing the fee.

Under the 1972 Order, the fee charged for conveyancing work (under the so-called 'Schedule II' method) is required to be:

> Fair and reasonable having regard to all the circumstances and in particular to
> (i) the complexity of the matter or the difficulty or novelty of the questions raised;
> (ii) the skill, labour, specialised knowledge and responsibility involved on the part of the solicitor:
> (iii) the number and importance of the documents prepared or perused, without regard to length;
> (iv) the place where and the circumstances in which the business or any part thereof is transacted:
> (v) the time expended by the solicitor:
> (vi) where money or property is involved its amount or value;
> (vii) whether any land involved is registered land within the meaning of the Land Registration Act 1925; and
> (viii) the importance of the matter to the client.

These guidelines are of course rather vague, and it was not

long before a case was brought in an effort to establish how these criteria were to be applied in practice. The case was *Property and Reversionary Investment Corporation Limited v. Secretary of State for the Environment* [1975] which involved the conveyancing charge in a case of compulsory purchase. The property price was £2.25 million and the vendors' solicitors' bill of £11,250 was referred for taxation. The bill was taxed at £4,625 but on appeal was raised by Donaldson J. to £5,500.

The interesting thing about Donaldson J.'s judgment is that he rejected the straightforward method of calculation that the taxing master had applied and argued that a 'broad look' (at p. 442) at the case was required. He described the search for a fair and reasonable sum as 'an exercise in assessment, an exercise in balanced judgment – not an arithmetical calculation'. It is instructive, before passing comment on this rather extraordinary claim, to examine the calculations that the taxing master had applied.

It had been agreed that 30 hours had been spent on the case. Multiplying this figure by an hourly rate of £15 and by a factor of 2 to allow for certain other aspects of the case, a basic fee of £900 was reached. To this was then added a further £3,120 in recognition of the value of the property (calculated as 0.5 per cent on the first £250,000 plus 0.1 per cent on the next £2m). This running total of £4,020 constituted the main item in the taxing master's figure of £4,625. Even the taxing master thus had contrived to raise the hourly rate charged from £15 to £154. A mere economist is lost for words!

When the Royal Commission on Legal Services came to make their recommendations about conveyancing charges (Royal Commission, 1979) they argued that scale fees, or 'standard' charges as they termed them, should be reintroduced. It is perhaps hardly surprising that the Commission should recommend a return to the practice of pre-1973 in the light of the judicial interpretation of the 1972 Order. Indeed, the Royal Commission took the opportunity to comment upon the judgment in *Property and Reversionary* in conjunction with two subsequent cases

(*Maltby v. D. J. Freeman and Company* [1978] and *Treasury Solicitor v. Regester* [1978]). In apparently approving these cases as support for the return to a system of scale charges they argued as follows:

These cases illustrated the impossibility of deriving any figure which can logically be explained by reference to any criteria except time and value . . . If conveyancing charges were based wholly on value there would be greater simplicity, [.] absolute certainty, which the public is entitled to expect, and no measure of injustice.

The task of determining 'standard' charges would be referred, under the Benson Commission proposals, to a Fees Advisory Committee. The issues therefore of whether cross-subsidisation within the scale of charges should continue and of how profitable conveyancing should be in relation to other types of legal work were thus not directly confronted. The implication that value rather than time be used as the central criterion inclines one to think that the Commission broadly approved of the system of charges as it had operated before 1973. One clue may reside in the following remarks:

So far as the solicitor is concerned it will not hurt him to take the rough with the smooth. Provided the charges are fixed by the Fees Advisory Committee both the profession and the public should be content.

This may be interpreted to mean that under the standard charge system unusually time-consuming cases will be rather profitable but will be offset by other less time-consuming cases rather than that high-valued transactions should generate high fees that will balance the low fees available on the conveyancing of cheap property. The Commission in their report lay great store by consumers being offered a perfectly predictable price for a transaction. Whilst it may be true that solicitors should be able to absorb the greater risk that scale charges throw back upon them, it is possible to argue that such a move would undermine competitive forces and thus ensure that consumers pay a high fee for sure rather than take their chances.

The proposal for a return to a system of scale charges has not so far been implemented, although as we have already argued property value seems in practice to be a more important criterion in determining charges than does the amount of time taken. Applying the arguments developed in earlier chapters about the economics of taking care, one is driven to the conclusion that the premium currently being charged to traders in high-valued property seems to be excessive. The compulsory liability insurance that solicitors now have to take, in conjunction with the observation that a more highly-valued property should be dealt with more carefully (and thus probably in a more time-consuming fashion), combine to suggest that there is no compelling reason why property value should play the dominant role that it does at present. It may be a useful rule of thumb to include the value of property in back-of-the-envelope estimates, but an efficient allocation of solicitor resources would be better served by basing fees on the amount of time taken by a case.

The size of the profession and conveyancing fees

One of the important consequences of the high degree of reliance upon conveyancing, already alluded to, is that the incomes of the solicitors' profession taken as a whole may be relatively sensitive to changes in property market conditions. The volume of turnover in the market is reasonably volatile because the number of properties changing hands and the relation between property prices and prices generally tend to rise and fall in sympathy with one another. Variation from year to year in incomes resulting from property market fluctuations may express itself not only in profit levels but also in things like the number of articled clerks taken on by practices. When the property market is booming one might expect an expansion in recruitment and vice versa. In order to establish whether such a hypothesis has any validity one may compare various measures of property market turnover with figures for recruitment. The requisite raw data are set out in Table 12.2.

Economic Aspects of Legal Services

TABLE 12.2 PROPERTY MARKET CONDITIONS AND THE
RECRUITMENT OF SOLICITORS

Year	Average house price (current prices) £ col.1	Average house price (at 1966 prices) £ col.2	Number* of property transactions '000 col.3	Mortgage advances: net commitments '000 col.4	Number of articles registered col.5
1966	3,850	3,850	.	.	1,520
1967	4,080	3,980	.	.	1,613
1968	4,340	4,045	.	.	1,531
1969	4,660	4,120	.	.	1,707
1970	5,000	4,156	.	.	1,739
1971	5,650	4,293	.	719	1,856
1972	7,420	5,262	.	727	1,914
1973	10,020	6,506	109	512	2,423
1974	11,100	6,212	97	472	2,481
1975	11,787	5,312	103	683	2,414
1976	12,704	4,915	113	706	2,730
1977	13,650	4,556	125	788	2,535
1978	15,594	4,807	128	784	2,983
1979	19,925	5,146	.	705	2,814
1980	23,596	5,437	.	695	1,711

Note: *Figures are monthly totals: figures for 1973 & 1974 refer to October, whilst figures for other years are for November.

Sources: col.1: Housing and Construction Statistics, London, HMSO.
col.2: as for col.1 plus the Retail Price Index from *Economic Trends*, London, HMSO.
col.3: 'Trends in Land Sales', *Economic Trends*, March 1980 (figures only available for 1973 – 79).
col.4: as for col. 1; no figures available pre – 1971.
col.5: Law Society (private communication) plus 'Survey of Legal Education', *Journal of the Society of Public Teachers of Law*, July 1975.

It is difficult to claim unambiguous support for the hypothesis, since this would require a higher degree of correlation between movements in the real value series (measured either as column (2) or column (2) multiplied by column (3)) and in the number of recruits (column (5)). As other columns show however movements in the overall value of sales mask independent movements of real house prices (that is of house prices deflated by the retail price index) and of the number of properties changing hands. The number of houses bought will depend upon the availability of mortgages (inter alia) and this will in turn be influenced by the volume of funds which building societies have available. Thus the number of properties traded may decline even though the average price of property is rising in real terms as indeed happened in 1973. Changes in house prices relative to other prices and in the number of properties traded may have different effects on conveyancing fees. If conveyancing fees are related to nominal property values, then real income from conveyancing will rise if (for example) the number of houses traded remains the same but house prices rise relative to prices generally.

If it is not possible to claim clear support for the hypothesis, it is nevertheless possible to suggest that the large number of recruits taken on in 1973 owed something to the property market boom of 1971 and 1972. It is possible also to suggest that the contraction of the property market in 1980 and 1981 will leave its mark. The squeeze on profits that the collapse in volume of turnover will have occasioned (unless there was a wide-spread, large increase in conveyancing fees in relation to house prices) would suggest that many practices will be under pressure. This pressure may express itself both through a fall in recruitment and also through the emergence of unemployment amongst qualified solicitors. The recruitment figures for 1980 have to be treated with some caution because of changes in the Law Society examination rules, but even allowing for such adjustments seem to be on the low side and thus consistent with a property market slump. Further evidence comes from the suggestion by the President of the Law Society at the Society's 1980 conference that unemployment amongst solicitors was beginning to emerge and that the profession should beware of continuing to recruit relatively large numbers.

CONTINGENT FEES

For the remainder of this chapter we turn to a suggestion for reform in England, urged by some commentators, which would radically alter the lawyer/client relationship and might have a significant effect on the income earned from litigation. Although such income represents only a small proportion of total income in England, it is probably significantly more important in the United States of America. According to the NBPI, all 'court work' and 'advice and negotiation on contentious matters' contributed a total of 16.1 per cent towards income in 1966 – 67. Since the figures for Court work cover criminal as well as civil cases, the relevant proportion will actually be considerably lower. Indeed, one of the claims made by supporters of the call to introduce a contingent fee system in England is that it would widen the range of instances in which individuals would feel inclined to press claims for damages. Any such expansion might thus be expected to raise the gross incomes of solicitors.

The essence of the contingent fee system is that the risk of losing a case is shifted from the client to the lawyer. In the event of winning, the plaintiff pays a previously agreed proportion of his damages to his lawyer by way of a fee, whilst if the case fails and no damages are awarded, no fee is payable. Under this system both parties will generally be responsible for their own legal costs, irrespective of the outcome of the case. The net result is that the plaintiff cannot end the day worse off than he was at the start, even though the price he pays for this luxury is a reduced proportion of any damages that are agreed or awarded. The fact that personal injury claims cases are heard by juries in the United States rather than by a judge as they are in England tends to cloud the debate about whether a contingent fees system should be adopted in England. This fact is not germane however to the central issue of how lawyers' fees should be paid.

As far as the individual with a tort claim is concerned, the question of whether a contingent fee arrangement promises to be a superior way of financing the claim as compared with a fee-for-service arrangement depends upon several things. In addition to depending upon the reputation of the lawyer engaged to handle the case, the assessment of the best fee arrangement will be influenced by:

(i) the client's perceptions of the probabilities associated with winning and losing the case, and with the different amounts of damages that might be awarded in the event of winning;

(ii) the client's attitude towards risk, since under the contingent fee system there is less variability between the wealth levels associated with winning and losing the claim;

(iii) the relation between the detailed terms of the payment contract with the lawyer, particularly the size of the fixed fee that would be charged under a fee-for-service contract and the proportion of damages payable under a contingent fee system;

(iv) any information the client may have about the lawyer's attitude towards risk, since those lawyers who are relatively averse to risk may be inclined to settle at an earlier stage than others;

(v) the clients's wealth level at the start of the case, since the wealthy might be more inclined to take risks than the poor and thus be more inclined to opt for fee-for-service arrangements.

By using the economic theory of behaviour under uncertainty, it is possible to produce an analytical picture of this choice between financing arrangements as it confronts both lawyers and their clients. Space limitations preclude a detailed discussion of this analysis, but the main conclusions are relatively straightforward, and include the following, all of which are based upon the assumption that clients are risk averse:

(i) the higher the level of the fixed fee and the higher the level of prospective damages the more likely is it that a contingent fee system will be preferred, other things being equal;

(ii) the higher the probability associated with winning the case the less attractive the contingent fee system, other things equal;

(iii) the higher the proportion of damages payable in fees, the less attractive the contingent fee system, other things being equal;

(iv) the greater the degree to which the risk aversion of clients exceeds that of lawyers the more attractive will be the contingent fee system, although the lower the degree of risk aversion amongst clients the smaller will be the merits of the contingent fee system, again, holding other things constant.

Contingent fees for litigation, like scale fees for conveyancing shift risks from clients to lawyers. Whilst it is generally possible to identify instances where individual clients would prefer to take the risks themselves, it does seem plausible to argue that in both cases lawyers are best-equipped to absorb such risks provided that they are dealing with a sufficiently large number of cases for the risks to even themselves out. But as is clearly seen from the conveyancing fee debate, the shifting of risk is not the only matter at issue. What is important is whether there is competition between solicitors over the fees or terms that they charge, irrespective of whether the fees or terms are fixed in advance. Lawyers may find it easier to attract customers if they offer fixed fee services, but equally may find it expedient to offer the customer a choice between a fixed fee and a variable fee. Fixed fee contracts do not require that a scale of standard charges be set down, but merely that clients be given the opportunity to express their preferences one way or the other. It is difficult to resist the conclusion, put forward by Lees (1966) and others, that the elaborate regulatory protection afforded to the legal profession restricts the ability of clients to express their requirements.

CONCLUDING REMARKS

In this chapter we have discussed some of the economic aspects of the provision of legal services. The treatment has been highly selective and has concentrated on solicitors and on the method of charging for conveyancing work. Amongst the important issues we have not discussed at all have been the division of the legal profession between barristers and solicitors, the provision of legal services in the context of commercial law and the role of the Law Society.

There can be little doubt that the number of solicitors currently practising and the pattern of income and expenses they enjoy both reflect the protection from competition afforded by the staute preventing those other than solicitors from charging for conveyancing services. Efforts to preserve this monopoly and its value are discernible over a long period. The system of land registration, designed to simplify the process of buying and selling land, has taken a long time to develop, and Offer (1977) has argued that the resistance to the introduction of the system was led by those concerned to protect the interests of the legal profession. In any event, conveyancing continues to contribute disproportionately to the income of solicitors despite pressure from others who would like to break into the conveyancing field. This protection has the effect of making life more comfortable for solicitors, particularly those in provincial practices, than it would otherwise be and encourages the continued, rather uneasy, existence of cross-subsidisation between different classes of legal work. Both these deviations from a competitive solution encourage a misallocation of resources within the legal profession, between the legal profession and other sectors, and in the economy at large because of the high costs of land transactions that result.

FURTHER READING

Zander (1976, 1978) is a good starting point for discussion of the provision of legal services. For a more thorough discussion of the notion of 'unmet legal need' see Morris, White and Lewis (1973). The use of cross-subsidisation by solicitors is criticised by Lees (1966). Further comments on solicitors' earnings are to be found in Bowles and Phillips (1977). The suggestion that the English legal profession have systematically resisted the introduction of land registration in order to maintain their income levels is explored by Offer (1977). The more general question of the consequences of allowing the legal (and other) professions to be essentially self-regulating has attracted increasing interest, particularly from economists: see for example Benham and Benham (1975).

Bibliography

Ackley G. (1978) *Macroeconomics: Theory and Policy*. New York: Macmillan.

Adelstein R. (1981) The Plea Bargain in England and America: A Comparative International View. Burrows & Veljanovski (Eds) (1981) *post*.

Akerlof G. (1970) The Market for Lemons: Qualitative Uncertainty and the Market Mechanism. *Quarterly Journal of Economics*, 84, pp. 488 – 500.

Anderson R.W. (1976) *The Economics of Crime*. London: Macmillan.

Asimakopulos A. (1978) *An Introduction to Economic Theory: Microeconomics*. Oxford: Oxford University Press.

Atiyah P.S. (1979) *The Rise and Fall of Freedom of Contract*. Oxford: Clarendon Press.

Atiyah P.S. (1980) *Accidents, Compensation and The Law*. 3rd Edn. London: Weidenfeld and Nicolson.

Atiyah P.S. (1981) *An Introduction to the Law of Contract*. 3rd Edn. Oxford: Clarendon Press.

Averch H. & L. Johnson (1962) Behaviour of the Firm Under Regulatory Constraint. *American Economic Review*, 52, pp. 1053 – 69.

Bailey E.E. (1973) *Economic Theory of Regulatory Constraint*. Lexington, Mass.: Lexington Books, D.C. Heath & Co.

Baldry J.C. (1974) Positive Economic Analysis of Criminal Behaviour. A.J. Culyer (Ed) (1974) *Economic Policies and Social Goals*. London: Martin Robertson.

223

Baldus D.C. & J.W. Cole (1975) A Comparison of the work of Thorsten Sellin and Isaac Ehrlich on the Deterrent Effect of Capital Punishment. *Yale Law Journal*, 85, pp. 170 – 86.

Baldwin J. & M. McConville (1977) *Negotiated Justice*. London: Martin Robertson.

Baldwin J. & M. McConville (1979) *Jury Trials*. Oxford: Clarendon Press.

Bank of England (1967) The UK Exchange Control: A Short History. *Bank of England Quarterly Bulletin*, 7, pp. 245 – 60.

Bank of England (1981) The Effects of Exchange Control Abolition on Capital Flows. *Bank of England Quarterly Bulletin*, 21, pp. 369 – 73.

Barber W.J. (1967) *A History of Economic Thought*. Harmondsworth: Penguin.

Beale H. (1980) *Remedies for Breach of Contract*. London: Sweet and Maxwell.

Beale H. & T. Dugdale (1975) Contracts between businessmen: planning and the use of contractual remedies. *British Journal of Law and Society*, 2, pp. 45 – 60.

Beccaria-Bonesana C. (1767) *An Essay on Crimes and Punishments*. London: Almon.

Becker G.S. (1968) Crime and Punishment: an economic approach. *Journal of Political Economy*, 76, pp. 169 – 217.

Benham L. & A. Benham (1975) Regulating Through the Professions: a perspective on information control. *Journal of Law and Economics*, XVIII, pp. 421 – 447.

Bishop W. (1980) Negligent Misrepresentation through Economists' Eyes. *Law Quarterly Review*, 96, pp. 360 – 79.

Bowles R. (1980) Juries, Incentives and Self-selection. *British Journal of Criminology*, 20, pp. 368 – 76.

Bowles R. (1981) Mortgages and Interest Rates: an economist's view. *New Law Journal*, 131, pp. 4 – 5.

Bowles R. & J. Phillips (1977) Solicitors' Remuneration: a critique of recent developments in conveyancing. *Modern Law Review*, 40, pp. 639 – 50.

Bowles R. & C.J. Whelan (1979) The Currency of Suit in Actions for Damages. *McGill Law Journal*, 25, pp. 236 – 43.

Bowles R. & C.J. Whelan (1981a) International Contracts: English Law and Floating Exchange Rates. *National Westminster Bank Review*, November, pp. 27 – 36.

Bowles R. & C.J. Whelan (1981b) Judicial Responses to Exchange Rate Instability. Burrows and Veljanovski (Eds) (1981) *infra*.

Bowles R. & C.J. Whelan (1981c) Judgment Awards and Simple Interest Rates. *International Review of Law and Economics*, 1, pp. 111 – 14.

Branson W.H. (1979) *Macroeconomic Theory and Policy*. 2nd Edn. New York and London: Harper and Row.

Brown J.P. (1973) Toward an Economic Theory of Liability. *Journal of Legal Studies*, 2, pp. 323 – 49.

Burrows P. (1979) *The Economic Theory of Pollution Control*. Oxford: Martin Robertson; Cambridge, Mass.: MIT Press.

Burrows P. & C. Veljanovski (Eds) (1981) *The Economic Approach to Law*. London: Butterworths.

Calabresi G. (1970) *The Costs of Accidents: a legal and economic analysis*. New Haven: Yale University Press.

Calabresi G. (1975) Optimal Deterrence and Accidents. *Yale Law Journal*, 84, pp. 656 – 71.

Calabresi G. (1977) The Problem of Malpractice: trying to round out the circle. *University of Toronto Law Journal*, 27, pp. 132.

Calabresi G. & P. Babbitt (1978) *Tragic Choices*. New York: W.W. Norton & Co.

Calabresi G. & A.D. Melamed (1972) Property Rules, Liability Rules and Inalienability: one view of the cathedral. *Harvard Law Review*, 85, pp. 1089 – 1128.

Carr-Hill R.A. & N.H. Stern (1979) *Crime, the Police and Criminal Statistics*. London: Academic Press.

Carter R.L. (1974) *Theft in the Market*. London: Institute of Economic Affairs.

Chiang A.C. (1974) *Fundamental Methods of Mathematical Economics*. 2nd Edn. Kogakusha, Tokyo: McGraw-Hill.

Coase R.H. (1937) The Nature of the Firm. *Economica* n.s. IV, pp. 386 – 405.

Coase R.H. (1960) The Problem of Social Cost. *Journal of Law and Economics*, 3, pp. 1 – 44.

Cranston R. (1977) Creeping Economism: some' thoughts on law and economics. *British Journal of Law and Society*, 4, pp. 103 – 15.

Culyer A.J. (1973) *The Economics of Social Policy*. London: Martin Robertson.

Diamond P.A. (1974) Single Activity Accidents. *Journal of Legal Studies*, 3, pp. 107 – 64.

Diamond P.A. & E. Maskin (1979) An Equilibrium Analysis of Search and Breach of Contract, I: Steady States. *Bell Journal of Economics*, 10, pp. 282 – 316.

Diamond P.A. & J.A. Mirrlees (1975) On the Assignment of Liability: the uniform case. *Bell Journal of Economics*, 6, pp. 487 – 516.

Ehrlich I. (1972) The Deterrent Effect of Criminal Law Enforcement. *Journal of Legal Studies*, 1, pp. 259 – 76.

Ehrlich I. (1973) Participation in Illegitimate Activities: a theoretical and empirical investigation. *Journal of Political Economy*, 81, pp. 521 – 65.

Ehrlich I. (1975) The deterrent effect of capital punishment: a question of life and death. *American Economic Review*, 65, pp. 397 – 417.

Elliot D.W. & H. Street (1968) *Road Accidents*. Harmondsworth: Penguin.

Furmston M.P. (1981) *Cheshire and Fifoot's Law of Contract*. 10th Edn. London: Butterworths.

Gibbs J.P. (1975) *Crime, Punishment and Deterrence*. New York: Elsevier.

Glover J. (1977) *Causing Death and Saving Lives*. Harmondsworth: Penguin.

Harris D., A.I. Ogus & J. Phillips (1979) Contract Remedies and the Consumer Surplus. *Law Quarterly Review*, 95, pp. 581 – 610.

Harrod R.F. (1951) *The Life of John Maynard Keynes*. London: Macmillan. Reprinted in 1972 by Penguin.

Heal G. (1977) Guarantees and Risk-sharing. *Review of Economic Studies*, XLIV, pp. 549 – 60.

Hirsch W.Z. (1979) *Law and Economics: an introductory analysis*. New York: Academic Press.

Hirshleifer J. (1976) *Price Theory and Applications*. London: Prentice Hall International Inc.

Home Office (1979) *Evidence submitted to the Inquiry into the United Kingdom Prison Services.* Volume 1, Paper IIC(1). London: HMSO.

Jarrell (1978) The Demand for State Regulation of the Electric Utility Industry. *Journal of Law and Economics*, 21, pp. 269.

Jones-Lee M.W. (1976) *The Value of Life: an economic analysis.* Oxford : Martin Robertson.

Kitch E.W., M. Isaacson & D. Kasper (1971) The Regulation of Taxi-cabs in Chicago. *Journal of Law and Economics*, 14, pp. 285 – 350.

Knott J.A. (1980) Foreign Currency Judgments in Tort: an illustration of the wealth-time continuum. *Modern Law Review*, 43, pp. 18 – 35.

Kronman A.T. (1978) Mistake, Information and the Law of Contracts. *Journal of Legal Studies*, 7, pp. 1 – 34.

Kronman A.T. & R.A. Posner (Eds) (1979) *The Economics of Contract Law.* Boston: Little-Brown.

Lancaster K. (1974) *Introduction to Modern Microeconomics.* 2nd Edn. Chicago: Rand McNally Publishing Company.

Landes W. (1971) An Economic Analysis of the Courts. *Journal of Law and Economics*, 14, pp. 61 – 107.

Landes W. (1973) The Bail System: An Economic Approach. *Journal of Legal Studies*, 2, pp. 79 – 105.

Landes W.M. & R.A. Posner (1978) Salvers, finders, good samaritans and other rescuers: an economic study of law and altruism. *Journal of Legal Studies*, 7, pp. 83 – 128.

Law Commission (1978) *Report on Interest.* London: HMSO. Cmnd. 7229.

Law Commission (1981) *Foreign Money Obligations.* Working Paper 80. London: HMSO.

Layard R. (Ed) (1972) *Cost-Benefit Analysis: Selected Readings.* London: Penguin.

Layard P.R.G. & A.A. Walters (1978) *Microeconomic Theory.* London and New York: McGraw-Hill.

Lees D.S. (1966) *Economic Consequences of the Professions.* London: Institute of Economic Affairs.

Leibenstein H. (1966) Allocative Efficiency vs. X-Efficiency. *American Economic Review*, 56, pp. 392 – 415.

Lipsey R.G. (1979) *An Introduction to Positive Economics*. 5th Edn. London: Weidenfeld and Nicolson.

MacAvoy P.W. (1971) The Regulation-Induced Shortage of Natural Gas. *Journal of Law and Economics*, 14, pp. 167 – 99.

Macaulay S. (1963) Non-contractual relations in business: a preliminary study. *American Sociological Review*, 25, pp. 55 – 69.

Macneil I.R. (1974) The Many Futures of Contracts. *Southern California Law Review*, 47, pp. 691 – 816.

Macneil I.R. (1978) Contracts: adjustments of long-term economic relations under classical, neoclassical and relational contract law. *Northwestern University Law Review*, 72, pp. 854 – 965.

Macneil I.R. (1981) Economic Analysis of Contractual Relations. Burrows and Veljanovski (Eds) (1981) *op. cit.*

Major W.T. (1980) *Sale of Goods*. 4th Edn. London: Macdonald and Evans.

Mann F.A. (1971) *The Legal Aspect of Money*. 3rd Edn. Oxford: Oxford University Press.

Mann F.A. (1976) Case note of Miliangos. *Law Quarterly Review*, 92, pp. 165 – 68.

Martin D.L. (1972) The Economics of Jury Conscription. *Journal of Political Economy*, 80, pp. 680 – 702.

Miller R. & J.B. Wood (1979) *Exchange Control For Ever?* London: Institute of Economic Affairs.

Mooney G. (1977) *The Valuation of Human Life*. London: Macmillan.

Morgan R. & R. Bowles (1980) Fines: the case for review. *Criminal Law Review*, 1981, pp. 203 – 14.

Morris D. (Ed) (1979) *The Economics of Consumer Protection*. London: Heinemann.

Morris P., R. White & P. Lewis (1973) *Social Needs and Legal Action*. London: Martin Robertson.

NACRO (1981) *Fine Default*. Report of NACRO Working Party.

National Board for Prices and Incomes (1968) *Remuneration of Solicitors*. Report no. 54. London: HMSO. Cmnd. 3529.

Needleman L. (1976) Valuing other peoples' lives. *Manchester School*, 44, pp. 309 – 42.

Niskanen W. (1971) *Bureaucracy and Representative Government.* Chicago: Aldine.

North P.M. (1979) *Cheshire and North's Private International Law*, 10th Edn. London: Butterworths.

Offer A. (1977) The Origins of the Law of Property Acts 1910 – 25. *Modern Law Review*, 40, pp. 505 – 21.

Ogus A.I. & G. Richardson (1977) Economics and the Environment: a study of private nuisance. *Cambridge Law Journal*, 36, pp. 284 – 325.

Ogus A.I. (1973) *The Law of Damages*. London: Butterworths.

Peltzman S. (1973) An evaluation of consumer protection legislation: the 1962 drug amendments. *Journal of Political Economy*, 81, pp. 1049 – 91.

Peltzman S. (1975) The effects of automobile safety regulation. *Journal of Political Economy*, 83, pp. 677 – 725.

Phillips J. (1976) Economic Deterrence and the Prevention of Industrial Accidents. *Industrial Law Journal*, 5, pp. 148 – 63.

Phillips J. & K. Hawkins (1976) Some economic aspects of the settlement process: a study in personal injury claims. *Modern Law Review*, 39, pp. 497 – 515.

Phillips J., K. Hawkins & J. Flemming (1975) Compensation for Personal Injuries. *Economic Journal*, 85, pp. 129 – 34.

Pigou A.C. (1932) *The Economics of Welfare*. 4th Edn. London: Macmillan.

Posner R.A. (1974) Theories of Economic Regulation. *Bell Journal of Economics and Management Science*, 5, pp. 335 – 58.

Posner R.A. (1977) *Economic Analysis of Law*. 2nd Edn. Boston: Little-Brown.

Posner R.A. (1980) A Theory of Primitive Society with Special Reference to Primitive Law. *Journal of Law and Economics*, XXIII, pp. 1 – 53.

Posner R.A. & A.M. Rosenfield (1977) Impossibility and Related Doctrines in Contract Law: an economic analysis. *Journal of Legal Studies*, 6. Reprinted in Kronman and Posner (Eds) (1979) *op. cit.* pp. 122 – 38.

Public Accounts Committee (1980 – 81) *Sixth Report of the Committee of Public Accounts*, Session 1980 – 81, HC 226, Home Office. London: HMSO.

Pyle D.H. (1974) The Losses on Savings Deposits from Interest Rate Regulation. *Bell Journal of Economics and Management Science*, 5, pp. 614 – 22.

Pyle D.J. (1980) *The Economics of Crime and Law Enforcement*. SSRC Public Sector Study Group Bibliography Series no. 1 Public Sector Economics Research Centre, University of Leicester.

Rawls J. (1972) *A Theory of Justice*. London: Oxford University Press.

Riordan B. (1978) The Currency of Suit in Actions for Foreign Debts. *McGill Law Journal*, 24, pp. 422 – 41.

Rose F. (1979) *International Trade*. London: Sweet and Maxwell.

Rothschild M. & J. Stiglitz (1976) Equilibrium in competitive insurance markets: an essay on the economics of imperfect information. *Quarterly Journal of Economics*, 90, pp. 629 – 50.

Rowley C.K. (1973) *Anti-trust and economic efficiency*. London. Macmillan.

Rowley C.K. & G.K. Yarrow (1981) Property Rights, Regulation and Public Enterprise: the case of the British Steel Industry 1957 – 75. *International Review of Law and Economics*, 1, pp. 63 – 96.

Royal Commission (1978) *Royal Commission on Civil Liability and Compensation for Personal Injury*: Report. London: HMSO. Cmnd. 7054.

Royal Commission (1979) *Royal Commission on Legal Services: Final Report*. London: HMSO. Cmnd. 7648.

Shavell S. (1980) Damage measures for breach of contract. *Bell Journal of Economics*, 11, pp. 466 – 90.

Shaw S. (1980) *Paying the Penalty: an analysis of the cost of penal sanctions*. London: NACRO.

Shuster M.R. (1973) *The Public International Law of Money*. Oxford: Clarendon Press.

Silver A. (1974) Econometric studies in crime and deterrence: a survey. *mimeo*, City College, New York.

Simon H.A. (1959) Theories of Decision-Making in Economics. *American Economic Review*, 49, pp. 262 – 3.

Smith R. (1979) The Impact of OSHA Inspections on Manufacturing Injury Rates. *Journal of Human Resources*, 14, pp. 145 – 70.

Softley P. (1973) *A Survey of Fine Enforcement*. Home Office Research Unit, Paper 16. London: HMSO.

Softley P. (1978) *Fines in Magistrates' Courts*. Home Office Research Unit, Paper 46. London: HMSO.

Stigler G.J. (1970) The Optimum Enforcement of Laws. *Journal of Political Economy*, 78, pp. 526 – 36.

Stigler G.J. (1971) The Theory of Economic Regulation. *Bell Journal of Economics and Management Science*, 2, pp. 3 – 21.

Sugden R. & A. Williams (1978) *The Principles of Practical Cost-Benefit Analysis*. Oxford: Oxford University Press.

Swann D. (1979) *Competition and Consumer Protection*. London: Penguin.

Swimmer G. (1974) The relationship of the police to crime: some methodological and empirical results. *Criminology*, 12, pp. 293 – 314.

Tullock G. (1971) *The Logic of the Law*. New York: Basic Books.

Veljanovski C.G. & C.J. Whelan (1980) An Assessment of the Master Policy Indemnity Insurance Scheme. *New Law Journal*, 130, pp. 328 – 30.

Votey H.L. (1969) *Economic crimes: their generation, deterrence and control*. US Department of Commerce (PB), Washington, D.C.

Whynes D.K. & R. Bowles (1981) *The Economic Theory of the State*. Oxford: Martin Robertson; New York: St. Martin's Press.

Wilkinson H. (1980) Extortionate Mortgages. *New Law Journal*, 130, p. 749.

Williamson O.E. (1967) *Economics of Discretionary Behaviour: Managerial Objectives in a Theory of the Firm*. Chicago: Markham Publishing.

Williamson O.E. (1975) *Markets and Hierarchies: Analysis and Antitrust Implications*. New York: Free Press.

Williamson O.E. (1979) Transaction cost economics: the governance of contractual relations. *Journal of Law and Economics*, 22, pp. 233 – 61.

Williamson O.E. (1981) Contract Analysis: the transaction cost approach. Burrows and Veljanovski (Eds) (1981) *op. cit.*

Winch D.M. (1971) *Analytical Welfare Economics*. London: Penguin.

Winn Committee (1968) *Report of the Committee on Personal Injuries Litigation*, London: HMSO, Cmnd. 3691.

Wolpin K.I. (1978) An economic analysis of crime and punishment in England and Wales 1894 – 1967. *Journal of Political Economy* 86, pp. 815 – 40.

Woolley P.K. (1974) Britain's Investment Currency Premium. *Lloyd's Bank Review*, 113, pp. 33 – 46.

Zander M. (1976) *Cases and Materials on the English Legal System*. 2nd Edn. London: Weidenfeld and Nicolson.

Zander M. (1978) *Legal Services for the Community*. London: Maurice Temple Smith.

Index